MAXIMIZE! LEVERAGING THE STRENGTHS OF YOUR SMALL CHURCH

Ron Klassen has been a winsome and tireless encourager of small-place pastors and churches for decades. In this book, he draws on years of study and experience in order to help those who are part of small churches see that there are many advantages to smaller gospel communities. I was repeatedly encouraged and challenged as I read. This is a hopeful, positive, practical, and very encouraging book.

—Stephen Witmer
Pastor, Pepperell (Massachusetts) Christian Fellowship;
co-founder, The Gospel Coalition's Small Town Summits;
author of *A Big Gospel in Small Places*

There are healthy large churches and healthy smaller churches. There are also unhealthy examples of each. Yet it is true that although the vast majority of churches are small, the largest churches typically provide the examples we see expressed for effective ministry. Ron Klassen, a longtime advocate for small and rural churches, shows the hope we have in the small church by describing what a healthy small church looks like, what effective preaching sounds like, and what relational Christianity could be like when lived out in the context of a small church. It's an excellent book and worth your time!

—Ed Stetzer
Executive Director,
Billy Graham Center for Evangelism,
home of the Rural Matters Institute;
author of *Planting Missional Churches*

Ron Klassen's little book, *Maximize!*, is a goldmine! He draws on Scripture that speaks perfectly to the insecurities of small church leaders. His practical insights and ideas are drawn from years of conversations and observations about small churches. His writing is vivid and succinct. Klassen isn't just a cheerleader, he is a skilled, wise coach. I guarantee you will be helped!

—Lee Eclov
Retired pastor; grew up in a small South Dakota church;
author of *Pastoral Graces: Reflections on the Care of Souls*
and weekly columns for *PreachingToday.com*

In *Maximize!*, Ron Klassen has written a book about the value of small-church ministry that is deeply biblical, solidly practical, and eminently relatable. While reading it I found myself responding in two ways on a regular basis: nodding my head while thinking, "Yep, he gets what it's like," and then wrinkling my brow while wondering, "How did I not see that before?" The second response is especially true in the simple, yet profound ways that Ron unpacks biblical principles. If you serve in a small church, or if you serve small-church pastors, this book is required reading.

—Karl Vaters
Longtime small-church pastor, Cornerstone Christian Fellowship
(Fountain Valley, California); founder, *NewSmallChurch.com*;
author of *Small Church Essentials*

Ron Klassen has spent a lifetime of ministry developing the vision of a big God and significant ministry in settings of smaller towns and churches. Size should never be confused with the Spirit. Programming should never eclipse maturing people. With a combination of good theology and practical method, this is a guide to creatively "exploit" the unique opportunities in those smaller settings for maximum impact. This book is a real gift, and Ron was the right one to write it.

—Mark Bailey
Chancellor and Sr. Professor of Bible Exposition, Dallas Theological
Seminary; author of *To Follow Him: The Seven Marks of a Disciple*

I eagerly agreed to endorse this book because I deeply respect and admire my friend Ron Klassen. He's a profound thinker and a clear communicator. Then I read the book. All of it. In one night. I absorbed Ron's words like rain on my parched spirit which I didn't even know was dry. It turned out I desperately needed this book. This book showed me how to align my beliefs with God's nature and revelation. It will help me lead with greater courage and conviction because I see God and myself more clearly. Don't be surprised if God surprises you like He did me. Even more than a book about small-church ministry, this is a book about our gigantic God and the huge opportunity you and I have to glorify Him as we serve the people He loves.

—Phil Tuttle
President, Walk Thru the Bible; former small-church pastor;
author of *Crucible: The Choices that Change Your Life Forever*

For many years I've had the concern that small churches don't appreciate both the good they already have done and their potential. That's why I was so excited to read this book. Ron nailed it! Every small church pastor and leader should read this book, both for encouragement and for the valuable tips that will help maximize (or "exploit") the strengths of their small church. Reminding us of and encouraging us that the small church is all about relationships, Ron believes (as do I) that the small church is the best size for discipleship, and this occurs within the rich soil of intergenerational relationships. This book will be a rich resource for those thinking of small-church ministry and those already embarked upon what can be a rewarding and blessed ministry.

—Brian Wechsler
Director Emeritus, Village Missions;
former long-time small-town and small-church pastor

Ron is a proven leader and authority on rural church ministry. His previous book, *No Little Places*, is widely regarded as one of the leading books on rural ministry. His latest book, *Maximize! Leveraging the Strengths of Your Small Church*, is likewise an essential book for every pastor. It provides invaluable insight into how the size of the small church is not a hindrance but a springboard for effective ministry. I highly recommend anything that Ron has written and especially this new addition to the growing literature on the rural church.

—Glenn Daman
Longtime rural pastor, River Christian Church
(Stevenson, Washington); author of *The Forgotten Church*

Ron Klassen and I are ministry partners, and we've done small-town ministry together in a number of contexts over the years. I love his heart for pastors and churches in places many others overlook. In this book, Ron will help you discover how to exploit, not downplay or excuse, your strengths as a small church. This is a must-read primer for anyone involved in small-church ministry. Read this book and learn vital principles that are crucial for small-church ministry!

—Les Lofquist
Professor, Shepherds Seminary; former Executive Director of
IFCA International; grew up in a small Minnesota town;
former small-town church planter;
author of many church-related articles

MAXIMIZE!

Leveraging the Strengths of Your Small Church

BY
RON KLASSEN

Deep River
BOOKS

Cover design by Jason Enterline

ISBN—13: 9781632695895
Library of Congress Control Number: 2022935342

Printed in the USA
2022—First Edition
31 30 29 28 27 26 25 24 23 22   10 9 8 7 6 5 4 3 2 1

DEDICATION

To my wife, Roxy, the love of my life,
my primary adviser, and always steady no matter
how turbulent the seas of ministry.

TABLE OF CONTENTS

ACKNOWLEDGMENTS

I would like to express my special appreciation
to the following:

RHMA, which provided ample opportunities for
me to hone my thoughts about
small-church ministry, and graciously granted
me time to work on this book

Andy Carmichael and the Deep River Books team,
who provided their
expertise and encouragement, and who view
publishing as a ministry

The students in my Doctor of Ministry cohort
of rural and small-town
pastors, who read my manuscript and provided
superb insights

Countless small-church pastors and leaders whom
I have been privileged to meet over the years who
inspire me, serve as examples, and have processed the
contents of this book with me

PREFACE

I Have a Dream

For more than thirty years, ministry has taken me to hundreds of remote places all across the United States and Canada. Ironically, one of the most unique small towns I have ever encountered is within a few miles of where I live. Hopedale, Illinois, population 857, is largely a medical community. It has a thriving clinic, hospital, nursing home, and other senior housing. In fact, people regularly drive right by what is considered the premier downstate hospital (in Peoria) and travel the extra thirty minutes to the small town of Hopedale, where they seek medical help from the much smaller hospital there.

Ask Mark Rossi, until recently the chief operating officer of Hopedale Medical Complex, for a tour, and you will hear him sing its praises. He will tell you how patients are known by name, how each patient's primary doctor closely oversees all their care, and how each person who enters their doors gets more attention because there is a lower staff-to-patient ratio. He will show you state-of-the-art equipment and assure you that the medical team is cutting-edge in all they do. He will tell you about a surprising array of services that they offer—considerably more than you would expect. And then the clincher: he will take you into one of the hospital rooms and show you the view out the large

window—beautiful, serene countryside that serves as a healing balm for each patient who occupies that room.

Somewhere on the tour, Mark will also tell you: "We *exploit* the fact that we are small and rural."

Exploit. Not *downplay.* Not *excuse.*

Exploit captures the heartbeat of what you will be reading in pages to come. As you read, I hope you will become absolutely convinced that small size is not an inherent liability but a trait begging to be exploited. I hope you will see that small churches have advantages, and that they are well-suited to fulfill God's mission for your church. I hope you will see the good in *your*-sized church.

Too often, far from exploiting, we are prone to see weaknesses and limitations—to compare our small-sized church with bigger churches and conclude that we come up short. Too often we try to emulate the big church, and by doing so we obscure our own church's strengths and make it look weak in comparison.

This book is the outcome of an unfolding dream many years in the making. This dream began to crystallize about twenty years ago when my then-grade-school daughter Catrina was given an "I have a dream" homework assignment in honor of Martin Luther King Day. Working with Catrina, I couldn't help but ask myself what big dream I would like to see fulfilled, should God choose to work through me. I penned these words:

> I have a dream. I envision small churches all across the country that are not trying to imitate large churches, but study themselves and their communities, and then prayerfully design ministries uniquely suited for their size, place, and time.

The ministry God has entrusted to me affords plenty of opportunity to stoke this dream, because much of it happens in small places and is church-centered. Because of this, the pages that follow will have somewhat of a small-town slant. But I am confident that small churches in cities will glean much help and encouragement as well.

After you complete this book, my hope is that you will be motivated to become more intentional about maximizing the strengths of your small church, and become anxious to *exploit* its virtues!

SECTION ONE

ALIGNING OUR THINKING WITH GOD'S

INTRODUCTION

"Jack" recently arrived in Smallville. A month ago, he graduated from seminary. Like about half of new pastors in small towns, Jack grew up in the city where he had attended a large church. His seminary was also located in a city, and most of his professors taught from an urban, large-church point of view.

Jack is thousands of small-church pastors, including me. Years ago, God in His sovereignty plucked my wife Roxy and me out of a big place and put us into a small one. Small town. Small church. Somewhat unwittingly, I went about trying to make my small church into a big church, mainly because that's what I knew. This proved to be an exercise in futility, in part because I don't have the skill set to be a large-church pastor. But also, it was because there were only about six hundred people in our entire thirty-five-square-mile county, the sixth least populous county in the continental United States, with about one person per every two square miles—hardly fertile ground for a large church!

Also somewhat unwittingly, I wanted my church to be like a big church because I had a big-is-better mentality. I figured that if we couldn't be big in size, we could at least be big in practice. Fortunately, my congregation was patient with me. And, they were good teachers. Thus began my journey of discovery about healthy small-church ministry.

Statistics vary,[1] but it is safe to say that a majority of churches in the US today have fewer than a hundred in attendance each week. About 95 percent of churches have fewer than five hundred in attendance. In other words, only about 5 percent of pastors are serving churches of medium to large size. The vast majority of pastors will never serve a church larger than 150 people. Perhaps this means we are mislabeling—maybe, instead of *small*-size churches, we should call them *normal*-size churches. For sure, if many of us are in it for life, we do well to make sure we have right thinking about small-church ministry. And, we do well to work at becoming small-church specialists.

Where to start? Theology is the place. *Theos* is the Greek word for "God"; *logia* means "study of." Therefore, *theology* simply means the study of God—His perspective, His truth. For our purposes, we are looking at a theology for small churches. Our problem is that we often look at our small churches from our perspective and not God's, which can leave us short-sighted and discouraged. We do well to hone what David Ray insightfully calls "a small theology."[2]

This first section of this book is meant to help align our thinking with God's. These chapters are critically important. Please take time to allow them to nourish your mind, heart, and soul.

Good theology will take us to practical outcomes. That's what we'll discuss in Section Two of this book.

Before we go any further, I want to insert a couple of disclaimers. First, while I say lots of good things about small churches,

---

[1] I am reluctant to cite a source for church attendance because sources vary so much, and because church attendance is very much in flux today. In other words, any statistics I cite will likely be obsolete by the time you read them. Suffice it to say that there are many small churches in the US.

[2] David Ray, *The Big Small Church Book* (Cleveland: The Pilgrim Press, 1992), 7.

nothing I've written is meant to be anti-big church. I believe big churches have an important place in Christendom today. I think there are lots of virtues of big churches. I still think very highly of the big church I was a member of years ago in Phoenix. I can easily sing the praises of big churches—but that's material for another book.

Second, this is not meant to be an anti-church-growth book. My hope for any church, no matter what size, is that it grows in one way or another. It's very possible that if your church applies some of the things in this book it will grow—at least in depth, if not in breadth.

This book's concern is not about what size is best, but about how to be *your* best, whatever size your church is.

CHAPTER ONE

SMALL CHURCH DOESN'T MEAN LESS OF GOD

Their place of worship had been torn down. They wept as they looked at the much smaller foundation of the new building that was to replace the old. This was one more painful reminder of significant population decline, one more reminder that family and friends had been forcibly removed from them and that they would not likely in their lifetimes again experience a large gathering of worshippers in their community.

You may be thinking I'm describing your situation. After all, about half of the rural counties in the US have lost population in the last ten or so years. In some places, the highway has bypassed a town. In others, a manufacturing business or coal mine has closed. For many, technology has replaced manpower on the farm. Small population is one of many reasons why churches are small.

Actually, the description above comes from Zechariah's day, nearly 2,500 years ago. A small percentage of those who had inhabited Israel years earlier had just returned from captivity. Soon they began rebuilding the temple. At first, they were highly motivated because it had been many years since they had worshipped together. But when the foundation was completed, the old-timers wept (Ezra 3:12). A foundation tells one thing: size. These folks who had remembered Solomon's temple looked at the footprint of what was to be their new temple—and with the assumption that big is better, concluded the new temple would be inferior.

Questions inevitably surface in situations like this: Can our worship be as meaningful? Can our youth ministries be as effective? Does reduced size mean reduced spiritual vitality? Should we lower our expectations to match our size? Sometimes we don't respond very well to questions like these. In Ezra's day the discovery that their temple would be smaller sent them into a tailspin, and for the next fifteen years the foundation just sat there. They apparently concluded that no temple was better than a small temple.

It is because of this halted construction that God raised up Zechariah. The prophet tells of a vision he received from the Lord of a completed, functioning temple (Zech. 4). Zechariah predicted that this temple would be completed during the administration of Zerubbabel, the governor at that time (Zech. 4:7).

Small Church, Big God

The stage is set for a couple of theology lessons. Aligning the people's perspective with God's proved to be the impetus needed to get the Jews back to work. And history tells us they did indeed complete the temple during Zerubbabel's administration.

Zechariah's theology lessons provide much-needed perspective for those of us today who worship in small churches. His words resonate for those of us who may at times find ourselves intimidated, with feelings of inferiority, or discouraged—especially if we play the comparison game with big churches, if our church is located in the shadow of a megachurch, or if we've attended conferences or read books, articles, or blogs in which big churches capture the spotlight.

The crux of Zechariah's theology emerges in two verses. First, Zechariah reminds the people that regarding the temple—and I think we can rightly say there is application here for the church— it's not human might or power that is important but whether the Spirit of God is at work.

> This is the word of the LORD to Zerubbabel: "Not by might, nor by power, but by my Spirit, says the LORD of hosts" (Zech. 4:6).

Every square foot of the former temple—the big temple, Solomon's temple—had exhibited human might and power. About 153,600 men had worked on that temple for seven years (2 Chron. 2:17), at who knows what cost. It ended up being a massive, palatial temple. But Zechariah says, "You know what? It's not human might or power that matters. It's whether God's Spirit is working inside, bringing life, health, and vitality to the congregation." There was little evidence of God's Spirit at work in Solomon's temple, especially during its latter days.

Do small churches get less of God? Can small churches be as spiritually vital as large churches? Theology lesson #1: God does not dole out His Spirit in proportion to the size of the church. Buildings may be huge, people may be attending in droves, but the working of the Holy Spirit does not depend upon externals like these. Our challenge is to resist the kind of thinking that leads us to conclude that big is better.

This truth has been reinforced time and again through my forty-plus years of small-church ministry. A few years ago, I did some interim preaching for a small church. It didn't take long for me to be impressed by their warmth, spontaneity, enthusiastic worship, laughter, tears, hugs, and eagerness to receive the Word of God. It wasn't their building that impressed me. Nor were their services executed flawlessly. What I found striking was their vibrancy and health. The Spirit of God was clearly evident in their midst!

Because this church is a couple of hours from our home and my family had commitments in our own church, they didn't go with me on those Sundays when I was preaching. After each visit, I'd tell Roxy and our kids what I had experienced. Soon curiosity got the best of them and on a free Sunday they went with me. My family saw the church to be everything I had said it was. While driving home, Roxy commented, "I would enjoy being a part of this church as much as a church of a couple thousand." These were not empty words; Roxy had grown up in a church of a couple thousand. I share this not to speak disparagingly about big churches (as I said earlier, I'm not an anti-big-church guy) but rather to underscore Zechariah's words: spiritual vitality is not proportionate to size.

No Little People, No Little Places

Theology Lesson #2 emerges a few verses later. Remember, Zechariah here is trying to lift Israel out of their doldrums so that they will get back to building the temple. Doing so, he predicts: "Whoever has despised the day of small things shall rejoice" (Zech. 4:10).

"Small things" here refers to the anticipated small temple and its ministries. The Hebrew word for "small" referred not only to size but also to what many considered insignificant; in other words, it was a description of how the Jews were feeling about their new temple. Frankly, it's also a description of how many feel today about small churches. The Hebrew word for "despise" means to hold as insignificant, belittle, or regard as unimportant. Merrill Unger says this verse "challenges one who would look down upon something small in which God is glorified."[3] Zechariah predicts that the people will find joy during this new season of ministry in a small temple.

Most anyone who has been in small-church ministry for some years will attest to periods of time when few big things happen. Maybe it's because we are in a small place where it seems big things almost never happen. More likely, it's because of the dailiness of ministry.

Adding to the difficulty of living with the dailiness of our ministry, we may hear or read about other places, maybe a big church down the road a ways, where big things seemingly happen continuously. We find ourselves discouraged because this kind of stuff isn't happening in our church. While it is always good to reflect and as best we can make sure we are not doing something that might hinder God from working, often we simply need to realize that big things are exceptions; that's why they get publicity. If a teacher has a good but ordinary Sunday school class, that isn't likely to make news. Normal day-in, day-out ministry doesn't get a lot of press. But that's where the vast majority of ministry is. Zechariah encourages us to not despise periods of time when seemingly only small, ordinary things are happening in our church. And, he reminds us that much joy can be found in the small.

This period of time could be a long time. The "day" Zechariah alluded to stretched on for more than four hundred years.[4] Some

---

[3] Merrill F. Unger, *Zechariah: Prophet of Messiah's Glory* (Grand Rapids: Zondervan Publishing House, 1963), 77.

[4] "Day" here refers not to a twenty-four-hour day but a period of time. For example, we might say, "We live in a day of increasing costs for health care."

of you might be thinking, "What a coincidence. That's exactly how long I've been teaching my Sunday school class!"

I venture to say that many of us can count major excitements on our fingers. But think about this: it is ordinary, daily ministry, collectively over time, that is likely to make the bigger difference in people's lives. Very few receive lasting impact from one big, exciting ministry event. It might give us a quick charge; it might be the talk in our church and community for a time, but chances are the excitement will soon fizzle and life will be back to the daily routine. Think how you have been most impacted. Has it been through an exciting event or through the day-in, day-out faithful ministry of people in your church?

Years ago, a Scottish pastor of a small village church was known and loved for the way he continually encouraged people. When he died someone noted, "There is no one left to appreciate the triumphs of ordinary folk."[5] Are we encouraging each other in the daily things folks are doing in our church?

Are we prone to despise small things? God doesn't. The words of renowned theologian and apologist Francis Schaeffer capture God's perspective so well: "In God's sight there are no little people and no little places."[6]

Reflecting God's Perspective

How might we despise small things? I've identified ways that I have been prone to do so. First, we might despise small when we don't prepare as much for a smaller number. We've all been there, haven't we? Do we slack off on preparation—for a Sunday school

---

[5] John MacArthur, *The MacArthur New Testament Commentary: 1 Corinthians* (Chicago: Moody Press, 1984), 351.
[6] Francis Schaeffer, *The Complete Works of Francis Schaeffer*, Vol. 3 (Wheaton, IL: Crossway Books, 1974), 60.

class, worship service, Bible study, or kids' club—if we know that not many will be showing up? If we somehow know there are going to be a hundred more in attendance next week, would we do a better job of preparation? There is a distasteful tendency in many of us, myself included, to not work as hard if we know fewer are going to be present.

Second, we might despise small things by jumping to conclusions based upon size alone. We might look at a large church and assume it has a better worship service or youth ministry. Is bigger always better? Would you rather live in a mansion with an abusive spouse or a simple farmhouse with a loving spouse? We need to avoid jumping to conclusions based on size alone, as the people in Zechariah's day did.

Third, we might despise small things when we assume that limited resources—like people, finances, and buildings—translate into inferior ministry. The story of Gideon tells us otherwise (Judg. 6–8). As he was busy trying to muster a big army God told him, "You've got too many men." God's work doesn't get done just because we manage to scrape together all the workers we think we need. Doing so, we are operating under the might-and-power philosophy Zechariah discredits.

We might assume that limited money limits what God can do. Sometimes being small means we don't have all the electronic bells and whistles that bigger ministries have. Maybe our building isn't as up-to-date. What is God incapable of doing because of our limited resources? Again, the story of Gideon helps get our thinking on track. He not only tried to amass a large army but also a large cache of weapons. God said, "Put away your weapons; you're going to win this battle with trumpets, pitchers, and torches."

Can we have a good children's ministry if our resources are the equivalent of trumpets, pitchers, and torches? I was struck by a video produced by Awana, a children's ministry, that showed kids in a foreign city playing games on a makeshift circle on a busy street. Every few seconds the kids had to clear the street to let a car pass. How much facility do we need? Throughout history God has often delighted in turning the tables upside down by doing big things with small resources. As the song says, "Little is much when God is in it."

Now, the assumption here is that laziness or stinginess are not at issue. If we are short-staffed because of unwilling workers, or if the church facility is inadequate because we are not giving as we are capable, that's another problem. But if we are doing what we can and still end up short, God is more than able to make up the difference.

Our perceived limitations are opportunities to depend upon the Lord. They are opportunities to demonstrate God's ability rather than ours. And, they provide opportunities to praise God for results that clearly came from Him!

Fourth, we might despise small things when we assume small size translates into small results. In 1 Chronicles 21, we find David taking a census before deciding whether to lead his men into battle, though God had specifically told him to go. One of the severest disciplines of God resulted, leaving seventy thousand of David's army dead. David had relied too much on human might and power and not enough on God. David was reminded that God can multiply resources a hundred times. Christ proved this when He multiplied five loaves and two fishes (Matt. 14:14–21). If we extrapolate the "hundred times," we'll conclude that a church of fifty can accomplish what one might think it would take a church of five thousand to do! God might take a well-placed small offering and use it to win thousands. The next world-changer might be attending your kids' ministry.

This happened when Philip the evangelist had a ministry with just one Ethiopian at a lonely rural outpost (Acts 8:26–40). Years later, when missionaries arrived in Ethiopia, they found widespread Christianity, reportedly because of Philip's ministry to just one person. Wouldn't it be something if one person in your church was someday used of God to reach an entire nation? Stories abound of small churches being used of God to nurture youth who became world-changers.

An anonymous quote that captures the gist of this chapter goes something like this: "If you ever think you're too small to be effective, you've never been in bed with a mosquito." Every church, regardless of size, has limitless potential because it can draw from infinite resources.

Do not despise small things. Don't moan and groan about small size. Rather, find joy. There's so much good in small churches. Find it. *Exploit* it. This is the message of Zechariah.

Evidently King David, who earlier had taken his census, learned his lesson. Sometime later he wrote, "Some trust in chariots and some in horses, but we trust in the name of the LORD our God" (Ps. 20:7).

When we get caught up in the we're-too-small syndrome, the real issue might be theology, not size. When we find ourselves asking nagging questions about our small churches, we need to remind ourselves of God's perspective.

In my favorite *Peanuts* cartoon, Lucy and Linus look out the window at a steady downpour. "Boy," says Lucy, "look at it rain. . . . What if it floods the whole world?"

"It will never do that," Linus replies confidently. "In the ninth chapter of Genesis, God promised Noah that would never happen again, and the sign of the promise is the rainbow."

"You've taken a great load off my mind," says Lucy with a relieved smile.

"Sound theology," states Linus, "has a way of doing that!"

Hopefully a sound *small theology* will lead us to the settled conviction that "in God's sight there are no little people and no little places."

FOR REFLECTION

1. How has the population changed in your community in recent years? Is it growing or declining? Is the makeup of the people about the same or different? Has population change resulted in significant pain for some? Encouragement for others?

2. How do you measure health, vitality, and success in your church? What evidences are there of God's Spirit working in your midst?

3. Look up synonyms for "small" and "big." How do these inform us about whether we are prone to despise small things?

4. Looking back on your life, have you been impacted more by one or two significant events or through the day-in, day-out faithful ministries of others?

5. Who in your church has a long track record of faithful ministry that collectively, over time, has made a big difference in people's lives?

6. Where do you find joy in your *small thing* (church)?

CHAPTER TWO

THE SMALL CHURCH IS THE TOTAL PACKAGE

I wasn't a small-church pastor long before shortcomings became evident. We couldn't assemble a choir. We couldn't have a women's ministry. We couldn't offer a program for youth. We couldn't do much-needed building improvements. The *couldn'ts* were winning, or so it seemed.

I arrived with a list of prerequisites for how to *do* church, but some of them weren't *doable*. Reality forced me to evaluate my assumptions. I was drawn back to the early church, which often met in homes (e.g., Acts 5:42; Rom. 16:5; 1 Cor. 16:19). Believers met in homes not because they were opposed to gathering in public buildings but because they weren't usually welcome in temples or synagogues. These fledgling groups of believers didn't yet have time or resources to build places for worship.

Taking Our Cues from Small, New Testament Churches

Significantly, much church practice that is followed today by small and large churches alike came out of these small, house-church settings. Some of us as students spent a lot of class time learning about how to *do* church from Acts 2:42–47, where we find believers breaking bread, fellowshipping, praying, holding Bible studies, giving, evangelizing, and worshipping—where?—much of it in homes. These were perhaps most often the homes of wealthier people such as Philemon, which would typically include courtyards and even upper rooms, perhaps large enough for between fifty and a hundred people (Philem. 1–2).[7] Interestingly, the average first-century church size was perhaps about seventy-five, which is about the average size of churches today. It is texts like these that led David Ray to the conclusion that "small churches are the right size to be and do all that God calls a church to be and do."[8]

The church at Colossae is a case in point.[9] It was located in a once-thriving city, but its population had gradually declined until the historian Strabo, just a few years before Paul wrote his letter to the Colossians, referred to it as a "small town." Colossae had previously been prosperous because it was located on a main trade route, but its fortunes changed when this road was rerouted and Colossae was bypassed. By Paul's day, the Colossian church was located in the smallest town of all the churches he wrote to in the New Testament. You may be in a similarly declining community. (If you are, and need some encouragement, you will find it in the epilogue of this book.)

---

[7] See also Acts 12:12–17, where we find "many" believers gathered (v. 12). It says Peter knocked at the "door of the gateway" (v. 13), which indicates they could have been meeting in the outer courtyard.

[8] David Ray, *The Big Small Church Book* (Cleveland: Pilgrim Press, 1992), 18.

[9] I am grateful to Les Lofquist, from whom I first heard insights about the small town of Colossae and the small church located there, in a seminar years ago. This seminar contributed seminal thoughts that have greatly aided the development of my own small theology.

As in other communities in that day, the church at Colossae met in a home (Philem. 2). This makes a prominent theme in Paul's letter to them quite striking—the theme of fullness, completeness, perfection, and maturity (synonyms, essentially). We see this in Colossians 1:28: "Him we proclaim . . . that we may present everyone mature in Christ."[10] Looking through the lenses of a small church in a small town (declining, even), it seems ironic that of all the places Paul wrote, it was here that he says maturity in Christ is attainable. Paul tells us the small church is the total package; it is the right size to fulfill all that God calls the church to be and do.

Every biblical purpose for the church can be fulfilled just as well in a small church as in a large church. We might be prone to think, "How can our small church, with so many shortcomings and inadequacies, possibly produce full, complete, and mature Christians?" Colossians indicates it is possible. In fact, as you read Section Two of this book, you may conclude that for some aspects of Christian living and growth, the small church may be the more optimum size.

Let's Make This Practical

A small church's youth group with just a handful of students, meager budget, no youth pastor, and no gym can just as effectively produce Christian maturity in teens as a large-size group in a big church. In fact, might it be more effective? The small church's worship services can be just as glorifying to God, and just as edifying and meaningful, even if it doesn't have a worship team or a lot of skilled musicians. The preaching and teaching ministries of small churches can be just as impactful, even if the preacher doesn't have the skills to match some of the megachurch giants. Its outreach can be highly effective, even if it isn't able to produce the attractional

---

[10] This theme thread is also found in Colossians 1:9, 19, 25; 2:2, and 9–10.

services or programs found in large churches. Colossians indicates that small size need not diminish any of these. Keep reading, and you may even conclude that small size is something to *exploit!*

Very important: small churches do not need to wait to grow to a certain size before they can be all that a church should be, like a child waiting to grow to a certain size. If so, some have no hope of becoming complete or full. With only a few hundred residents within a thirty-mile radius of our former church in Nebraska, there was little hope that our church could ever become medium-sized, much less large. Does this mean there was no hope for us to become mature? Colossians indicates otherwise.

Piling on the Evidence

Saying it another way: while there may be many appealing things about large churches, there is no evidence that large churches are able to more effectively produce mature believers. I am intrigued by the findings of Christian Schwarz, widely regarded as one of the top church-health assessment experts in the world. After much research, worldwide in scope, he concluded:

> Those familiar with church growth literature regularly encounter the names of a number of large churches which are held up as models to be imitated. The presupposition is that *large* churches are by definition *good* churches. Is this thesis tenable? Our research revealed for the first time that the opposite is probably true.[11]

---

[11] Christian A. Schwarz, *Natural Church Development; A Guide to Eight Essential Qualities of Healthy Churches* (St. Charles, IL: ChurchSmart Resources, 2000), 46.

Schwarz identified eight quality characteristics of healthy churches.[12] He found that, "On nearly all relevant quality factors, larger churches compare disfavorably with smaller ones."[13] In fact, the one exception is "inspiring worship service."[14] My understanding is that the data caught Schwarz by surprise. He did not begin with a bias toward the small church.

Another evidence: those who track the spiritual progress of children through adulthood have come up with a startling discovery—while big church youth programs may attract teens by the hundreds, the vast majority, when they leave high school, leave the church at a much higher level than youth in small churches. We'll say more about this later.

There is no evidence that people in small churches are more limited in their potential to become mature believers.

A Megachurch Pastor Speaks

Randy Frazee's book *The Connecting Church*, though written primarily with large city churches in mind, has some of the most encouraging words I have read about small churches.[15] When he wrote, he was a megachurch pastor. His book is the only admission I have seen in print from someone in a megachurch who says that the megachurch, unless it is intentional about some of its ministry approaches, will fall significantly short of small churches in producing Christian maturity. The reason for this, says Frazee,

---

[12] The eight qualities are: 1) empowering leadership, 2) gift-oriented ministry, 3) passionate spirituality, 4) functional structures, 5) inspiring worship service, 6) holistic small groups, 7) need-oriented evangelism, and 8) loving relationships.
[13] Schwarz, *Natural Church Development*, 48.
[14] Christian A. Schwarz, "The Strong Little Church," *Leadership*, Fall 1999, 54.
[15] Randy Frazee, *The Connecting Church; Beyond Small Groups to Authentic Community* (Grand Rapids: Zondervan, 2001).

is that much of what is needed to foster Christian maturity is lost when a church gets large, unless it is intentional about taking steps to be small.

Frazee goes much further than advocating small groups; he urges megachurch attenders to rediscover the concept of neighborhood. To accomplish this, he divided his congregation into communities, trying to recreate the dynamic that he sees happening in close-knit communities. He advocates such things as going on walks through the neighborhood, inviting neighbors into your home, doing Bible studies together, being accountable to each other, responding to each other's needs, and seeking advice from each other. He writes:

> [S]ociology experts point to the 1950s as a pivotal period in the development of a culture of isolation. It was during this era that Americans began to build places to live that have turned out to be more of a prison than a home—we know these places as *the suburbs*. . . . [A]ll you have in the suburbs is private space. People drive into their driveways, go into their houses, and never see one another. . . .

> [P]rior to the 1950s, designers placed residences, retail stores, and workplaces within walking distance of each other—and they did this, for the most part, for purely practical reasons. The kind of individualized transportation available to people today via the automobile was not available to prior generations. Yet, as it turns out, these densely created communities met more than practical needs; as a result of their layout, they facilitated our more basic and essential relational needs as well.

As we ponder the question of how to develop authentic Christian community we must carefully probe the obstacle presented by the places we have created in which to live. . . . [We] require [our] children to play in the back yard, which is surrounded by a six-foot privacy fence. When [we] go out for routine errands, [we] seldom encounter or relate to actual, real live people anymore. . . . [We] get gas at a station where there is no attendant. . . . [M]ost banking experiences . . . are automated. . . . When [we] venture to the . . . mall . . . [we] find ourselves surrounded by a multitude of people, but [we] know no one.[16]

Frazee concludes that we have "ignored what our ancestors had learned about designing a place where people could live together and grow in community."[17] He devotes his book to helping us envision how community can be recreated in city and big-church contexts. If you live in a small town, you would be especially encouraged by this fascinating book.

As I read, two thoughts surfaced. First, I was amazed to find a big-city megachurch pastor saying his kind of situation did not measure up to the dynamic of a healthy small church in a small town, apart from radical steps being taken. How refreshing! For years, many small-church and small-town people have been vainly trying to replicate a lot of the dynamics of megachurches. Here's a church trying to do the opposite. Second, it should be much more natural and easier to follow through on what Frazee is advocating in a small-church and small-town context.

---

[16] Ibid., 111–115.
[17] Ibid., 119.

No Limitations Here

The churches we served in Nebraska and Oklahoma adopted Colossians 1:28 as their theme verse: "Him we proclaim . . . that we may present everyone mature in Christ." We put this verse on our church's sign, in every Sunday's bulletin, on our church stationery, and in any other publicity materials. This verse stated our goal and purpose for being. It stated our belief that we had as much potential at progressing toward the goal of Christian maturity in our small setting as any church anywhere. Don't ever forget that these words were written to Colossae, a house church in the smallest of towns.

Exploit!

FOR REFLECTION

1. Can you identify a time when you've caught yourself thinking or saying: "We're just a small church"?

2. Can you identify ways that your church is proving to be an optimum size for fostering Christian growth and maturity?

3. Can you think of a time when you've been down on your church because it didn't measure up to the standards of a big church nearby?

CHAPTER THREE

THE SMALL CHURCH IS UNIQUE

Years ago, Lyle Schaller wrote a book titled *The Small Church Is Different.*[18] Just as the people in Zechariah 4 realized that their new small temple would be quite different from the previous big temple (see Chapter One), so today, as the title of Schaller's book reminds us, small churches are different from big churches.

Swimming or Running?

I have benefited greatly from several books David Ray has written on small-church ministry. A story he tells about a duck hunter drives home the point of this chapter. The duck hunter got a new retriever who, when commanded to fetch a stick thrown out on a pond, *ran* across the water. Wanting to show off his new remarkable dog, the hunter invited his friend out for a demonstration. The hunter threw, gave the command, and the dog *ran* across the water and retrieved the stick. The hunter glanced proudly at his friend, who returned a noncommittal look. He threw the stick again and the dog retrieved it, but still his friend didn't seem impressed. Suppressing disappointment and irritation, the hunter

---

[18] Lyle Schaller, *The Small Church Is Different* (Nashville: Abingdon Press, 1982).

asked, "What do you think of my new dog?" With a rather disinterested tone his friend answered, "Your dog can't swim very well, can he?"[19]

Many today believe there is a "problem" with the small church: it doesn't "swim" very well. Some think that in order to be a good church, it has to be a good swimmer. Big churches swim—they're good. Could it be that the small church is a different dog, but not an inferior dog? Small churches may not swim very well, but what if they run? What if they get the job done just as well as churches that swim, only in a different way?

Now the big question: Should we try to teach that dog how to swim? Should we no longer allow it to run? A lot of time is devoted these days to trying to teach non-swimming churches how to swim. It happens in school classrooms, at conferences and seminars, in books, and in blogs. Might it be that swimming isn't the best way for some churches to get the job done? Might it be that some churches can do the job differently but with equally good results?

What I'm saying is that small churches do well to give themselves permission to operate differently from big churches. If we, as pastors and leaders, try to get our churches to function like big churches, we will always fall short. We'll be chasing a target we cannot attain. We'll be frustrated. And our people will likely be saying, "Why are we trying to be like them? Why can't we just be *us*?"

Different Approach, Same Purposes

Does this mean that small churches should try to accomplish different purposes than big churches? To carry the analogy further, the swimming and running dogs both accomplish the same thing:

[19] David Ray, *The Big Small Church Book* (Cleveland: The Pilgrim Press, 1992), 5.

they both retrieve the stick. So also, small and big churches should work toward fulfilling the same purposes. But, they might do so in different ways. Each should accomplish their purposes by catering to their strengths—*exploiting* their size, in other words.

By saying that the small church shouldn't emulate a big church, I am not trying to make a value statement. I'm not saying big-church methods are wrong any more than one would say a swimming dog is better than a running dog. Echoing Lyle Schaller, I am simply suggesting that the small church is unique. Because of this, it is good for small churches to study themselves and their communities, and then prayerfully design ministries uniquely suited for their size, place, and time.

Let's think about several possible ministry applications, some of which we will elaborate upon in future chapters.

Vision. Vision is important. But could it be that the way churches forge vision, communicate vision, and implement vision might differ from one context to another?

Small-group ministry. In recent years, there has been a lot of emphasis on small groups. It's no coincidence that the small-group movement has emerged simultaneously with the megachurch movement. But, is trying to implement a small-group ministry the way they do it in big churches the right thing to do? For one, a small church may already have a lot of the dynamics of a small group because of its size. If it is a good thing to do, and I think it often is, might the way it is most effectively done differ from how large churches do it? What happens, for instance, when one tries to force intimacy and transparency in a setting where people are fiercely private because there is no place to hide—where they are wary of long-term shame, should things they say in confidence leak out into the community? Many small-church—and especially small-town church—pastors and leaders have been frustrated in their attempts to implement small-group ministry.

Niche services. One church growth strategy, especially in city settings, has been to offer niche services: seeker, contemporary, coffee house, twentysomething, etc. I've had many conversations with pastors—especially small-town pastors—who have gone to seminars, gotten excited about a niche approach, tried to implement it, and it proved to be a church-emptying strategy.

Think for a moment about seeker services. They require two things: 1) anonymity, and 2) a large pool of seekers without which the service cannot be sustained from week to week. Almost certainly, neither of these are attainable in a small-town context.

Contemporary services also require at least two things: 1) Enough talent to put together a worship team and band. If this is only partially attainable, the small church can look inferior. 2) The ability to have homogeneity—the concept that you can grow a church when you cater to people with similar tastes. Small congregations, especially in small towns but even in larger settings, tend to be more heterogeneous, more diverse. One example of many: you are likely to find Grandma sitting beside her grandkids, who are in the service because there isn't a children's church.

Allow me to sound ridiculous in order to drive home a point: in the city, a successful church-growth strategy might be to offer a worship service that appeals to left-handed flute players who like Christian jazz music (I'm not even sure Christian jazz is a thing!). There is probably a "pool" of such people in the city who would be attracted to this kind of niche service. Try this in a small town, though, and it would be a church-emptying strategy! I share this example merely to reiterate that the small church is different. The very strategy that might lead to growth in one setting might produce the opposite result in another. One is swimming, the other running.

Youth ministry. There are lots of seminars and books, but how much of the methodology that is presented is swimming instead of running?

Preaching. Should we assume that preaching ought to be the same, no matter the size or context of the church? How many of us in preaching classes were taught that we might approach preaching differently in a small church?

These are the kinds of things we will explore in Section Two, as we move from theology to practical outcomes. These are also the kinds of things we will encourage you to *exploit!* Read on.

FOR REFLECTION

1. Can you identify ways that your church might be trying to imitate what large churches do instead of offering ministries that are uniquely suited for its size, place, and time?

2. What are the unique good things about your church that you should be exploiting?

3. If you never find yourself ministering in a medium- or large-sized church, how would you feel about yourself as a pastor/leader and as a person?

SECTION TWO

STRENGTHS-BASED MINISTRY

INTRODUCTION

Many small-church folks think their biggest issue is size, when in reality it's the need for a "small theology." Hopefully Section One has helped stir your thinking in this direction.

The best theology is not limited to lofty thoughts; it leads to practical outcomes. Once we've forged a small theology, we do well to discern how we might live out this theology in our church. How might the small church design ministries that will produce mature believers, as Paul told the Colossians was possible in their house church? How might the small church achieve the same end goal as the big church, but do it in a way suited for its size? How might small size actually prove to be an advantage rather than a liability?

The answer to questions like these lies with the small church maximizing its strengths while simultaneously minimizing its weaknesses. Taking it a step further, the answer is the small church coming to the place where it recognizes potential where many would see liabilities. The answer, as Karl Vaters says, is realizing that our small size is not a problem that needs to be solved but a strategic advantage God wants to use.[20] Instead of being problem-oriented, we need to be strengths-oriented. Instead of lamenting

---

[20] Karl Vaters, *The Grasshopper Myth* (Fountain Valley, CA: NewSmallChurch.com, 2012), 62.

the things big churches are doing that we cannot do, we do well to think about what small churches can do that big churches find difficult to do.

And then, *exploit* them! This is where we're going with Section Two of this book.

My hope, as you keep reading, is that you do not view this section as a recipe. Please don't read looking for two cups of this, one teaspoon of that, and then you will have cooked up a great small church. Please do not be looking for things to imitate that other churches are doing, big or small. Rather, consider what you are reading, consider the makeup of your church and community, and then prayerfully design ministries uniquely suited for your size, place, and time.

CHAPTER FOUR

THE MOST NOTEWORTHY STRENGTH OF THE HEALTHY SMALL CHURCH

Small-church people love being together. Ask what they like about their church and they will talk about it being friendly. They will have plenty of stories to tell about how they care for each other. Ask about their pastor and they may not even say anything about his preaching—they're more likely to tell how he is often seen around town mixing with people at all kinds of places and events, and how he was there for them at a difficult time in their lives.

Perhaps the most noteworthy strength of a healthy small church, commonly acknowledged by many, is that it is personal and relational. Relationships are highly valued in the small church.

What a contrast this is to big-church attenders who are more likely to talk about their church's well-executed three weekly worship services that attract different audiences, their recently completed building campaign, and a wide array of programs for children, teens, singles, divorced, alcoholics, and seniors.

Relationships Matter

This relational focus is what God desires for us as believers. Think about how much of the New Testament is devoted to encouraging healthy relationships. Think about the two greatest commands: love God, love others (Matt. 22:36–40)—both highly relational. Think about the "one anothers" of the New Testament—perhaps you've focused on them in your small group or worship service preaching. Think about the small church in the small town of Colossae being commended by the apostle Paul for its "love" for fellow believers (Col. 1:4).

Think about the plethora of relational texts in the New Testament. I've put together a montage of many of these texts:

> Live in harmony with one another . . . love your neighbor as yourself . . . pursue what makes for peace and for mutual upbuilding. . . . Let each of us please his neighbor for his good. . . . Thus, sinning against your brothers and wounding their conscience when it is weak, you sin against Christ . . . have the same care for one another. . . . Aim for restoration, comfort one another, agree with one another, live in peace. . . . If you bite and devour one another, watch out that you are not consumed by one another. . . . Let all bitterness and wrath and anger and clamor and slander be put away from you. . . . Be kind to one another, tenderhearted, forgiving one another . . . walk in love, as Christ loved us. . . . Do nothing from rivalry or conceit, but in humility count others more significant than yourselves . . . and may the Lord make you increase and abound in love . . . the Lord's servant must not be quarrelsome but kind to everyone . . . speak evil of no one, avoid quarreling, be gentle, and show perfect

courtesy toward all. . . . Let brotherly love continue . . . the wisdom from above is first pure, then peaceable, gentle, open to reason, full of mercy and good fruits, impartial and sincere. . . . Do not speak evil against one another… have unity of mind, sympathy, brotherly love, a tender heart, and a humble mind. Do not repay evil for evil . . . keep loving one another earnestly, since love covers a multitude of sins . . . let us not love in word or talk but in deed and in truth.

Think about how the Scriptures time and again make comparisons between church members and the relationships we have within our families, including extended families:

- Matthew 12:49–50—Jesus expands the definition of "family" by referring to His disciples as His mother and siblings.
- Galatians 6:10 (NIV)—"family of believers."
- 1 Thessalonians 2:7, 11—Paul compares his relationship to the Thessalonian church as being like that of a mother and father.
- 1 Timothy 1:2; Titus 1:4—Paul refers to Timothy as one of his children.
- 1 Timothy 3:5, 12—Paul tells Timothy that church leadership requires a kind of parenting, and so one of the qualities required of elders and deacons is that they manage their own households well—because, after all, the church is a family too.
- 1 Timothy 3:15—"household."
- 1 Timothy 5:1–2—Encourages intergenerational relating: older men with younger men, older women with younger

women, these different generations relating to each other as fathers and mothers, brothers and sisters.

- James 2:15—One of 231 texts that refer to church members as brothers and sisters in Christ.

This kind of family talk would have prompted first-century believers to sit up and take notice. No one in that day called someone a brother or sister who wasn't a blood relative. These descriptions meant exponentially more to people in that day than they do to you and me. Only in the New Testament is the Greek word *philadelphia* ("brotherly love") found outside the context of the home. Early Christians would have been shocked when they first heard this kind of family talk in reference to the body of Christ. Try to wrap your head around how radical it was when Jesus said of His disciples, "Here are my mother and my brothers. For whoever does the will of my Father in heaven is my brother and sister and mother" (Matt. 12:49–50).[21]

Perhaps the most amazing validation: Think about our God. Think about how He, before creating the world, set a relational example from eternity past. He is three persons—God the Father, God the Son, and God the Holy Spirit—in perfect relationship with each other. Think about how God throughout all of human history, beginning in the garden of Eden, demonstrated His desire to dwell with the people He created (Gen. 3:8). Later, He instructed the Jews to build a tabernacle and then a temple—both places for Him to dwell with His people (Ex. 25:8; 2 Chron. 6:1). Furthermore,

---

[21] For more information on the church being characterized as a family, see Lee Eclov's book, *Feels Like Home; How Rediscovering the Church as Family Changes Everything* (Chicago: Moody Publishers, 2019), 45–48. In these pages, he quotes other sources as well.

the psalmists repeatedly wrote about their desire to dwell in the presence of the Lord (e.g., Psalms 16; 84; 90; 132; 135; 140).

Think about our Lord when He was on earth. In John 10:14, He revealed Himself as the Good Shepherd, a key quality being that He knows His sheep and His sheep know Him. He wasn't known for starting ministries, constructing buildings, or launching programs. Rather, He seemingly always had people around Him. He was known for devoting considerable time to His twelve disciples, for traveling through the countryside where He constantly connected with people and had many wonderful conversations. He seemed to have a special affinity for people in need.

Relationships matter. We are designed by God to live in healthy relationships. Outside of our homes, where might this better happen than in a small church? In fact, as we continue, we'll make the case that without a strong relational orientation in our church, it is impossible for us to become the mature, complete Christians that Colossians says God desires us to be.

David Ray aptly writes:

> In a small church I will probably never be driven to my knees by architectural splendor. . . . I will probably never be stirred by the power and majesty of the music . . . the unison singing of hundreds of worshippers; I will probably never encounter preaching that overwhelms . . . and I will never have the assurance of being part of a mass movement, which is possible in large churches. However, in a small church I can experience a sense of family and community.[22]

---

[22] David Ray, *Small Churches Are the Right Size* (New York: Pilgrim Press, 1982), 55–56.

The healthy small church has a strong relational orientation. We do well to lean into this strength. We do well to discern ways this relational strength can be leveraged into other strengths, and how it can be the fuel that propels other strengths. This is what the chapters to come are all about. We'll offer suggestions for how this relational strength might be *exploited!*

FOR REFLECTION

1. One pastor said, "I am more motivated by creating a climate than by setting a direction." What do you think about this statement?

2. Are there any ways that your church needs to bring its behavior in line with its stated strength of "We're a friendly church"?

CHAPTER FIVE

MAXIMIZE THE STRENGTH: FOCUS ON PERSONAL RELATIONSHIPS MORE THAN QUANTITY OF RELATIONSHIPS

In a large church on a low-attendance Sunday, members will say, "We're missing a bunch of people today!" In a small church they'll say, "Hank is gone today. I wonder if his back is giving him problems again?" In a small church, "How are you?" is a sincere question, not just a greeting.

In the small church, there is a personal awareness and concern for individuals. People go to church each week wondering what has happened since last week to every other person in the church, and what their plans are for next week. As the song from *Cheers*, the once-popular television show, reminds us: people are drawn to places "where everybody knows your name."

Ministry Is Personal

Shawn McMullen, a small-church champion, writes this about his small church:

I know every member of our church personally. I know the parents and I know their children. I know the kids who attend our youth functions, and I know the names of those who have recently visited us. With few exceptions, I can stand at the door after a service and greet everyone I meet by name. Visitors are easily identified in smaller churches, and if the members are warm and friendly to newcomers, they will leave the service wanting to return.[23]

The parable of the lost sheep fits the small church (Matt. 18:12–14). The sheep that gets lost is immediately missed. The flock feels incomplete until the sheep is accounted for. This parable came to mind some time ago when I was attending a church picnic. One of the leaders called out, asking everyone to gather around. Then, he noticed someone had not yet arrived. He said, "Let's wait a few more minutes before we start."

Christ, the Good Shepherd, knows each of His sheep by name. The sheep also know His name and voice; He is not distant, not a stranger (John 10:1–5). Similarly, time and again the apostle Paul referred to people by name (e.g., Rom. 16; 2 Tim. 4:9–22).

The small-church pastor preaches to faces he knows. The big-church pastor looks out on a sea of faces, most of whom he doesn't know personally. Small-church pastors don't preach to crowds; they preach to individuals.

Think about what this statement means in a large church: "I love my congregation." Does it mean I love each person? Someone might say, "How can you say you love me when you don't know

---

[23] Shawn McMullen, *Releasing the Power of the Smaller Church* (Cincinnati: Standard Publishing, 2007), 20.

my name? When you didn't even call me when my father died? When you've never lifted a finger to help me with my needs or celebrate my victories?"[24]

A new member of a large church who had previously been in a small church was in the hospital. When a church staff member came to visit he said, "I'm glad you came, but I was hoping the preacher would come and see me." To this, the staff member quipped, "You don't want to be that sick!"[25]

Implications for Ministry

This "I know everyone by name" strength of the small church has the potential of translating into effective ministry. Youth ministry is a good example. It's easy to think that in order to have a good youth ministry we need programs, money, events, a band, gym, and lots of students. One of the major frustrations of small-church members is that they cannot offer what they think is a good youth ministry. But, to continue the analogy in Chapter Three, might it be possible to accomplish the same ends by running instead of swimming?

Think about the personal element that might be present in a small church's youth ministry, where the youth group consists of a handful of teens. Think about how people in the church know the youth and relate to them informally and spontaneously. I know of a small church where I am confident that if the youth are asked which adult in the church has most influenced them, the man who would win hands down is seventy-plus years old. He has no official youth position, but he connects with the youth each Sunday. They love to talk to him. They seek him out. During the

---

[24] Ibid., 12
[25] Ibid., 21

week, he often invites a couple of them out for pizza. He sends them notes in the mail—almost a lost art today.

Some time ago, I came across an article that told about a small-church pastor who was asked about his youth ministry. He paused, chuckled, then said, "You must be mistaken. We don't have a youth ministry!" But as his story unfolded, it became apparent that he *did* have a ministry with youth: he attended their ball games; during the week he spent one-on-one time with the teens who attended his church; he was intentional about talking to each teen at church on Sunday; he helped a single parent plan a birthday party for his teenage daughter. In the article a teen says this about his pastor: "Some of the best talks I had with my pastor were times we'd meet downtown while I was running errands for my mom. Pastor Johnson always acted interested in me and took time to talk. He cared about me outside the church walls."[26]

Did that pastor and church have a youth ministry? The pastor concluded he didn't because he didn't do it the way big churches do it. If we define youth ministry as "swimming," then his church didn't have a youth ministry. Is it possible to accomplish the same ends—to "run"—another way? Can one lead teens to Christ through a personal ministry instead of a program- or event-oriented ministry? Can one help teens grow in Christ through a personal discipling ministry instead of a program-oriented discipling ministry? Is there just as much possibility for a teen in this kind of situation to grow into a complete and mature Christian? In fact, might this kind of situation prove to be advantageous?

Truth is, we would probably make a mistake if we tried to do youth ministry in our small church like they do in big churches. Plus, we would feel defeated, because it's just not possible. At best,

---

[26] Joani Schultz, "How Small Churches Minister to Youth," *Leadership*, Spring 1985, 80.

we'll end up with a scaled-down version of what the big church is doing—and scaled-down means inferior. Why would youth want to be a part of an inferior ministry? Why not instead do something completely different, something that fits the relational strength of the church?

One couple in a small church decided to let teens know that their home was open to them every Thursday evening. They did personal discipleship (the wife with the young ladies, the husband with the young men). This was followed by food, games, and conversation around the kitchen table. These times led to discussions about all sorts of things, including important issues of life. Is this an inferior way to do youth ministry? How many youths in big churches get to spend this kind of individual quality time with their youth leaders?

Youth ministry is one example of many of the personal kinds of ministry that can be done in a small church. I am suggesting that we maximize this relational strength—leverage it into a ministry for youth that in turn becomes a strength of the church.

Phillip Gulley, in his typical compelling manner, writes:

> If you want to learn about life . . . take a paper route. I did . . . while in the fourth grade for the princely sum of seven dollars a week. As paper routes go, mine was small with only twenty-six customers. My friend Bill Eddy had upward of eighty customers and three times the income, though he was so frazzled, the larger wage seemed hardly worth the struggle. Bill needed the extra money to finance his pinball playing at Danner's Five and Dime.
>
> Having a limited clientele allowed me to learn . . . [about] each. If I had eighty customers, I would never

have gotten to know all these people. . . . I would have been consigned to a bicycle, flinging papers at porches as I whizzed by. Instead, I climbed off my bike and shook hands and learned of a wider world. It established a pattern for living which I've tried diligently to maintain—bigger isn't always better, more money means more worries, and knowing people beats knowing about them.[27]

Exploit!

FOR REFLECTION

1. Does your church have a youth ministry?
2. Are there any ways your church is trying to be a scaled-down version of a big church?
3. Describe examples of personal kinds of ministries that happen in your church.

---

[27] Philip Gulley, *Front Porch Tales* (Sisters, OR: Multnomah Books, 1997), 35–38.

CHAPTER SIX

MAXIMIZE THE STRENGTH: MAKE RELATIONSHIPS A HIGHER PRIORITY THAN PROGRAMS AND PLANNING

A pastor friend said, "Don't add stuff [i.e., programs]; just baptize what you already do and do it with non-Christians." In other words, if you hunt, take a non-Christian along. If you have a hobby, do it with a non-Christian. If you need to run to the grocery store, allow for extra time in case you run into a non-Christian. We don't need programs to be effective witnesses.

As you take walks around town, be intentional about stopping and talking to non-Christians. Recently, I met up with a church-planter friend who God was mightily using in his community. I asked, "So, what's the most effective thing you've done to reach people?" His reply, "I take my dog on walks."

This intentional, albeit unscripted, approach is actually in keeping with the Great Commission (Matt. 28:19–20). The literal translation of the first word is "going"—i.e. (paraphrasing), "As you are going about doing what you do, make disciples."

Am I suggesting that we shouldn't have programs, or that programs are not useful or important? Hopefully this is not what you are reading. I was a longtime Awana commander. Awana is a highly effective program for children. What I am saying is that in small-church ministry, we do well to make relationships a *higher* value than programs. We do well to be more relationship-driven than program-driven.

Valuing Relationships

Fleshing out this high value, we will likely find such things as:

Greater spontaneity. As you take walks, see this as a means to connect with neighbors; know you could end up on someone's porch for a discussion about an issue of life. On the spur of the moment after church, ask someone to come over for pizza and conversation. On a Saturday afternoon, encourage your son to text a bunch of kids, saying a pickup football game will be starting in thirty minutes at the school playground. Maybe you can throw together some snacks for a break.

In a social media post, a small-church pastor's wife wrote, "Anyone have a craft or project you are working on? Want to fellowship while working on it? I will be at the fellowship hall this Saturday morning from eight until noon if you want to join me with your craft/project. I'll turn on the coffee and you can come and go as you wish. Any takers?"

These kinds of things need not be programmed. They need not be found on the church's website or on its calendar weeks ahead of time. They need not be the result of someone's careful planning or scripted vision; they just happen in a healthy, relational context. Larger contexts tend to require more organization.

Greater availability. Be ready to drop everything to lend an ear, perhaps on short notice—or no notice. Have an open-door policy. Be easily accessible by phone. Be ready to drop everything to go get a cup of coffee. Being available makes us different in our small settings. A big-church pastor simply cannot be accessible. His office door is shut. Appointments are required. There's an administrative assistant between him and you.

A small-church pastor said, "It took me a long time to realize that interruptions don't take me from ministry; they are opportunities for ministry." Being available like this requires working ahead on sermons and such, so that interruptions don't put you in panic mode or pressure you into declining an invitation for coffee. I'll say more about this in a future chapter.

Greater frequency. One potential strength of healthy small churches is the amount of time members spend together outside of the regular church services. This mirrors Acts, where we find the early Christians day after day eating meals together with gladness (Acts 2:46). They enjoyed being together! Small churches are wired for this kind of repeated fellowship.

Relationships in small churches are a high value. Ask small-church members what really stands out about their church, and their almost reflexive answer is likely to be something like, "We're friendly. We care for each other."

A Caring Community

Think about how this relational orientation might translate into ministry that is every bit as effective (if not more so) as a large church's program orientation. Think about how we might care for each other in the church and people in the community. How do caring ministries tend to happen in large churches? How easy it is to think, "That's why we have a pastor for people care." Or, "We have a committee for that (e.g., a visitation committee or a funeral committee)." Or, "Let's start a program (for widows, single mothers, alcoholics, etc.)."

What tends to be the small-church way? Often, ministry happens more spontaneously and informally. Which is better? When you think about it, would you rather have a person show up with a meal at your front door because a committee is fulfilling their duty or because it comes from someone who has a personal concern for you? While we'd enjoy a visit from our pastor if we're in the hospital, wouldn't we be just as touched by someone who stops by simply because they care for us and not because it's expected of them to do so?

This healthy small-church orientation can be quite different from that of large churches. In small churches, everyone is viewed as a caregiver. There, people have time to care because they don't need to be fully occupied with keeping the institution running. There, personal caring can happen through everything they do together as a church: in worship services, Sunday school, during a church workday, etc.

Small churches are particularly the right size to be caring communities. Often this is expressed in very individual ways. Judy is the hugger. Sally sends birthday cards. Eight-year-old Tammy draws a picture and sends it to a person who is newly widowed. Bill is a carpenter who makes an outside ramp for a person who has just been confined to a wheelchair. Ellie is likely to show up on your doorstep with a casserole and pie. Caleb is good at saying a timely word in conversations. Robert shows up at a sick person's home with a lawnmower. All the "colors" in the small church blend together beautifully to form a tapestry of caring.[28] This tap-

---

[28] David Ray, *The Indispensable Guide for Smaller Churches* (The Pilgrim Press: Cleveland, 2003), 154–155, 157.

estry leverages the church's relational strength into a strength of caring for others.

In large churches, caring is likely to be superficial, sometimes hit-or-miss (perhaps because church staff aren't aware of needs or are overwhelmed by the number of needs), restricted to major crises, or considered to be the job of professional caregivers. But the church that is small enough for everyone to know everyone is small enough for everyone to care deeply and effectively for everyone.[29]

Another example of a caring ministry is what the professional world labels as counseling for those facing significant problems and challenges. How do big churches tend to help people with troubling issues? Very likely, they will have a staff counselor or they will send these folks to professional counselors. Randy Frazee writes,

> I would never want to imply that mental health profes-
> sionals are not needed to help us through some of the
> struggles we encounter in life. However, people often
> employ them as nothing more than a "paid friend." In
> my opinion, I would cautiously suggest that roughly
> eighty percent of this industry has been created in the
> last twenty-five years as an alternative to what true com-
> munity used to provide free of charge.[30]

Someone said, "When you've got a problem, you can either pay someone $150 an hour to help you or you can have a cup of coffee with a neighbor on his porch."

---

[29] David Ray, *The Big Small Church Book* (The Pilgrim Press: Cleveland, 1992), 17.
[30] Randy Frazee, *The Connecting Church; Beyond Small Groups to Authentic Community* (Grand Rapids: Zondervan, 2001), 129.

How do we care for people's lost souls? The gospel can be communicated through a program, or by attracting people to a church building, impressive worship service, or special event. Or, it can happen relationally.

How do we care for our members' spiritual growth? It can happen through dynamic preaching in an auditorium of three thousand, or through personal interaction over a Scripture text.

To again return to the analogy in Chapter Three: Can you see how one approach is swimming while another is running?

A Caution for Pastors

Taking it a step further: Can you see how this small-church perspective might put a pastor who doesn't share this perspective on a collision course with his church? Pastors often measure their leadership effectiveness by the number of programs they generate. A pastor may feel he needs to establish programs *or else we are not a real church.* Some of us pastors would do well to pause when we are tempted to react to a need by starting a program. We should be wary of trying to program everything. If good ministry is happening without a program, why risk killing it with a program?

Some time ago, Carl Dudley documented that program costs tend to increase with the arrival of a new pastor at the rate of about 25 percent of his salary. When the pastor moves on, many churches will not be in a hurry to replace him, opting instead for a period of calm and recovery. One denominational executive, somewhat tongue-in-cheek, went so far as to say that he could predict how much time a church would take between pastors based upon the number of new programs the previous pastor started![31]

---

[31] Carl Dudley, *Unique Dynamics of the Small Church* (Bethesda, MD: The Alban Institute, 1977), 17.

Programs are not the only way to do church. Programs might be trying to make a church swim when its forte is running. We need to be wary of gauging the success of a church by its programs.

FOR REFLECTION

1. How are you or others in your church "baptizing what we already do and do it with non-Christians"?

2. How might you or others in your church be more intentional about "baptizing what we already do and do it with non-Christians"?

3. What kinds of things happen organically in your church, and what kinds of things are better suited for programming?

4. In what ways do you personally minister to people in your church and community that are apart from any program?

CHAPTER SEVEN

MAXIMIZE THE STRENGTH: BE INTENTIONAL ABOUT INTERGENERATIONAL RELATIONSHIPS

There's a general rule of thumb: As churches get bigger, the likelihood increases that there will be more segregating of ages. Though small churches tend to combine ages out of necessity, my hope as you read this chapter is that your small church will move from necessity to theology—that you will lead them to the place where they value intergenerational ministry because it is a value of Scripture. And also, that your church will see intergenerational ministry as a strength, not a weakness. And even more, that your church will be intentional about making intergenerational relationships a centerpiece of its ministry.

Intergenerational Is Biblical

The primary reason we should value intergenerational ministry is because it is biblical. In Chapter Four, we showed that often a word picture for the church in the Bible is that of a family. Think about this: God has designed us to be in families with older and younger brothers, sisters, and cousins who relate to each other; there's a dad, mom, uncles, and aunts of a generation older, and there are grandparents of a generation older than them. In an extended family, you might be the only one your own age. Families are designed for intergenerational relationships.

This is the word picture God uses to describe the church. Yet as churches get bigger, there is a tendency to move away from this design unless there is an intentionality about doing otherwise. Bigger churches have a youth wing, children's wing, ministry for seniors, young couples' class, etc.

Intergenerational Is Beneficial to All

Could it be that God designed us to be in intergenerational relationships because of the benefits this affords us all? If so, how sad it is that small churches so often view their inability to provide a plethora of age-focused ministries as a liability. How sad to view this as a weakness when, in reality, it is a strength. How empowering it is when the small church views intergenerational ministry as a strategic advantage!

Hit the pause button for a minute and think of some benefits of intergenerational relating. What might older provide for younger and vice versa?

- Might we learn from those who have previously walked where we are presently walking? Is it possible that a small group made up entirely of adults in a similar life stage of raising teenagers is only pooling their ignorance when discussing parenting? Wouldn't there be an advantage to having some adults in the group who have been there, and who can share wisdom gleaned from their experience?

- Might the younger provide such things as joy, hope, and energy? Might it be a good thing for adults to get a dose of their idealism and enthusiasm? Might youth bring optimism for the future?

- Might the younger, in turn, benefit from the stories, history, and calm demeanor that the older can offer? Might they be inspired by years of faithfulness?

- Might the younger gain a better sense of belonging as older folks value them by taking an interest in their lives, listening to them sing and recite Bible verses, making themselves available for hugs, and having laps for toddlers to sit in?

- Might young parents be grateful for seniors who are like surrogate grandparents for their children every time they enter the doors of the church, and at different times throughout the week?

- Might *all* generations, by observing all this, begin to think less of their own preferences and to instead consider the preferences of others?

Psalm 145:4 wonderfully reinforces the value of intergenerational relationships found in small churches:

> One generation shall commend your works to another,
> and shall declare your mighty acts.

What a great aspiration for every small church. What better place than the small church to live out this psalm's reminder that no one generation can fully fathom the greatness of the Lord? (Psalm 78:4–8 is another wonderful text that strongly supports intergenerational ministry.) It takes different generations commending the Lord's works to each other.

Howard Hendricks, one of my seminary professors, used to say, "Every Timothy needs a Paul, and every Ruth needs a Naomi." I would add that every Paul needs a Timothy and every Naomi a Ruth.

Intergenerational Should Be Missional

Intergenerational relationships should be more than a default position because our church isn't big enough for a plethora of age-focused ministries—it should be a guiding principle for our ministry. It should be a strength of small-church ministry. It should be something we tout, not something that makes us defensive or apologetic. It should lead us to conclude that small size can actually enhance—not hinder—the spiritual development of its youth. *It should be missional.*

Intergenerational ministry as a modus operandi is more natural to fulfill in the small church. It is an advantage that small churches have over large.[32] In small churches, intergenerational ministry happens much more organically, while big churches have to work at making it happen. Randy Frazee realized this. When serving as a big-church pastor, he put much effort into incorporating intergenerational ministry into his church. Here are his own words telling us why:

> Many church leaders still believe that the most effective grouping of people is centered around the sharing of a common life-stage experience. While it may be the

---

[32] Brandon O'Brien, in his book *The Strategically Small Church* (Bloomington, MN: Bethany House Publishers, 2010), makes an especially compelling case for the value of intergenerational ministry. See pages 121–138. Some of his thoughts have strongly influenced my own thoughts in this chapter.

fastest way to grow a group of people numerically, it is not going to produce the best qualitative results in the lives of individuals.[33]

The Benefits Are Supported by Research

We should not be surprised to find that research supports this biblical approach. After many years of segregating by ages, large churches are realizing the weakness of doing ministry this way. When the younger generation moves through the church with little meaningful interaction with adults, the likelihood of remaining in the church when they outgrow youth ministry diminishes considerably.

Kara Powell, in her college transition project, tracked four hundred newly graduated high school students through their first three years of college. Her research led her to conclude, "There is a strong link between kids' involvement in intergenerational relationships and worship and their staying in church after they graduate."[34]

Much is said about the declining number of professing Christians in the US today. It is estimated that a significant proportion of this decline can be attributed to the dropout rate of those in their late teens and early twenties.[35]

Please read carefully the following quotes which offer clarion calls for intergenerational ministry:

---

[33] Randy Frazee, *The Connecting Church* (Grand Rapids: Zondervan, 2001), 194.

[34] Kara Powell, "Is the Era of Age Segregation Over?" *Leadership*, Summer 2009, 45.

[35] Thom S. Rainer and Sam S. Rainer, *Essential Church? Reclaiming a Generation of Dropouts* (Nashville: Broadman & Holman, 2008), 2.

Teenagers who experience only the youth group and never bond with others in the church are almost guaranteed to drop out [of church] after high school. If it's only the youth group that drew them, then only the youth group can hold them. No more youth group, no more kids. That's why I worked so hard to get our megachurch kids interacting with the rest of the church. But it was nigh unto impossible. Large churches tend to have an age-division paradigm that controls everything.[36]

It is a sad fact of life that often the stronger the youth program in the church, and the more deeply the young people of the church identify with it, the weaker the chances are that those same young people will remain in the church when they grow too old for the youth program. Why? Because the youth program has become a substitute for participating in the church. . . . When the kids outgrow the youth program, they also outgrow what they have known of the church.[37]

Simply put, we do teens a disservice when we segregate them from the life of the church. When we build youth ministries that don't fold students into the life of the congregation, the unintended consequence is a future of empty pews.[38]

---

[36] Dave McClellan, "The Small-Church Advantage," *Group*, January-February 1999, 34.

[37] Ben Patterson, quoted by Mark DeVries in his excellent book *Family-Based Youth Ministry* (Downers Grove, IL: InterVarsity Press, 1994), 117.

[38] Dave Wright, "Don't Segregate the Youth," The Gospel Coalition, http://thegospelcoalition.org/blogs/tgc/2013/09/17/dont-segregate-the-youth/print.

This sobering mountain of evidence has prompted Mark DeVries, a strong advocate of intergenerational youth ministry, to ask, "Could it be that the majority of our efforts in programming and publicity may, in fact, be moving teens away from rather than toward mature Christian adulthood?"[39]

There may appear to be advantages to youth ministries in big churches. We may look at what they do and be wowed by it. But what we see may only, at best, be a temporary advantage. Over the long haul, looking beyond the years of youth, the small church with its compulsion to assimilate its youth into the life of the church—with less programming and less glitz—may actually have an advantage.

Please don't misunderstand. I'm not saying churches shouldn't have age-focused ministries. There are developmental concerns that are best addressed at certain ages. Teenagers may have questions that they do not feel comfortable bringing up if their parents are in the room. There is value in age-appropriate teaching.

Besides, there's nothing to be gained by spending a lot of time debating age-focused ministries vs. intergenerational ministry. For most small churches, this is a pointless debate because it just isn't possible to do age-focused ministry to the same degree as large churches. Again, my desire is that we don't see this mixing of generations as negative or inferior. To the contrary, there is good reason to see it as an advantage. The small church is one of the few places left in American society where intergenerational relationships still exist. Instead of apologizing for this reality, let's *exploit* it!

Intergenerational in Practice

---

[39] DeVries, *Family-Based Youth Ministry*, 28.

Let's make this practical: A church cannot claim to have embraced intergenerational ministry simply because it has members of several generations sitting together in the Sunday morning worship services. Just being together isn't intergenerational ministry. We do well to think about how we might flesh this out.

One way is to design worship services so that all generations are engaged. My suggestion is to approach this as a tapestry that is woven together rather than a room that is compartmentalized. In other words, during the music portion of the worship service, weave worship songs together that relate to all ages. In sermons, weave stories, object lessons, and applications that apply to all ages. Utilize all ages as greeters and ushers, on the worship team, as Scripture readers, and among those who lead in prayer.

Viewing the church as a tapestry of ages woven together might prompt us to rethink having a time in every worship service when we invite all the kids up front for a story or having a token Youth Sunday once a year. What are we communicating when we compartmentalize like this? Might the children and youth think there are only certain times when the church is for them, rather than all the time?

We do well to encourage informal interaction between the younger and older. For several years, our then-grade-school-age daughter Charissa often connected with a seventysomething woman in our church. Charissa sought her out for hugs. This lady occasionally picked her up and took her out for lunch. When my daughter broke her arm, she received a card from this lady saying, "I'm going to miss your hugs."

Adults like these will enter children's lives when all ages are assimilated in the life of the church. When kids who are assimilated into church get too old for the youth group, they're going to have lots of other connections in their church, which provides hope that they will stay in the church.

Aaron Williams eloquently captures this priority of intergenerational relating:

> I learned from him [an older mentor in Aaron's life] that authentic ministry is intergenerational. He taught me that the church is at its best when the young and the old are integrated throughout the life of the congregation. Seniors must remember what it was like to be young, and the young must remember that they may one day become seniors. Therefore, we must be patient with one another. If we have a contemporary service for the young and a traditional for seniors, we teach the young and the old to be intolerant of one another. We are bordering on ageism. The young and the old must come side by side with each other and minister to the glory of God together.[40]

So, sooner or later you are going to get that phone call, with someone asking, "What kind of ministries does your church offer for children and youth? For young married couples? For seniors?" Please don't make this a time for an apology, or a time to sound

---

[40] Aaron Williams, "Intergenerational Ministry," *Kindred Spirit*, Spring/Summer 2011, 5.

defensive. Instead, *exploit* how your church values being an intergenerational family!

FOR REFLECTION

1. In what ways does your church shine when it comes to inter-generational relationships?

2. Are there some ways that your church might be more intentional about intergenerational relationships?

3. How is your church passing on the faith from one generation to the next? Where do you see this happening best?

4. How would you answer the person who asks, "What kind of ministries does your church offer for children and youth? For young married couples? For seniors?"

CHAPTER EIGHT

MAXIMIZE THE STRENGTH: EMPHASIZE THE ADVANTAGES OF RELATING WITH PEOPLE FROM ALL WALKS OF LIFE

S mall churches not only do less age segregation (last chapter); they also offer fewer niche ministries for people who are in special life circumstances. A pastor was asked a number of questions by a person who had just moved into the community:

> "How many ministries does your church have? Do you have a singles ministry?"
>
> "Yes, we do."
>
> "How about a ministry for those who are disabled?"
>
> "Yes."
>
> "For recovering alcoholics?"
>
> "Yes."
>
> "Twentysomethings?"

"Yes."

"Single parents?"

"Yes."

"Widows?"

"Yes."

"Wow! How big is your church?"

"Fifty-five."

We're All Brothers and Sisters Here

What's happening? In nearly every small church you will find couples, divorcées, disabled, alcoholics, and singles all relating to each other, supporting each other, and benefiting from each other's unique situations. There are no niche classes, small groups, or ministries for these folks. Instead, there is a church family that does life together, walking side by side with each other through all kinds of experiences. There is an intermixing of people from all walks of life, a grouping together, with everyone treated like everyone else. There is a reticence about allowing fellow church members' life situations to define their identity. Their identity is not defined by being single, disabled, or widowed; it is by being a fellow brother or sister in Christ.

Envision a thirtysomething man with Down syndrome singing his heart out as a member of the worship team. Envision a student chatting with a widow during the greeting time. Envision a divorced mom and mechanic visiting in the foyer, and in the course of conversation him asking if her car is due for an oil change. Envision a recovering alcoholic hugging a person who is struggling with infertility.

A friend of ours, a mother with three adopted special-needs children, posted this on Facebook:

> We are in a very rural area. In some ways, our small church is limited in how it can help us. Yet, they not just accept us but embrace us. When I've had to quickly get up and rush to the changing table in the middle of a service, I've seen their kind eyes. Many stop to ask how our week has been and commit to praying for appointments for us. Our pastor welcomes our daughter's vocalizations and has never made us feel like she isn't wanted in the service. They recently put sound out in the foyer so if we are having a rough morning we can at least hear the service out there while we care for our children.

To this post, a friend replied:

> Some of the most welcoming and accommodating churches I've heard of don't have a special-needs ministry. It's not about a program; it's about people. If the mindset is there, then a formalized ministry doesn't have to be. I love how your church is responding to your sweet girl! A lot of it is about figuring out how to creatively say "Yes" and "You're welcome here" and "We miss you when you're not here."

All Ministering to All

Might categorizing church people by life situations unintentionally create barriers? People might think, *If I go to this church, they will view me as disabled.* Or attenders might think, *We have a ministry for those with special needs, so I need not get involved.*

Taking it a step further: Might those who are in challenging life situations actually receive *more* benefit from being around people who are *not* like themselves? For instance, isn't it good for alcoholics to be around abstainers and not just other alcoholics? Some years back, a young lady had her driver's license revoked because of a DUI. (Actually, this wasn't the first time.) She went before the judge in court with an unusual request: Instead of going into another treatment program (she had previously been in several, without lasting results), could she fulfill her probation requirements by getting connected with a nearby small church? (She chose this church because it was within walking distance.) Her reasoning was that she needed to be around *healthy* people instead of people who were *unhealthy* like her.

This lady was able to work out a unique arrangement with the court whereby she would verify church attendance. Several in the church committed to developing a relationship with her, including a godly older woman who agreed to regularly report to the probation officer. She regularly met with her pastor and his wife. Beyond this, this small church did more than was being asked of them, including the assimilation of her young children into the church.

This lady was a part of that church for many years, during which time she grew in her walk with God. She is alcohol-free. She is driving again. She is a testimony to the kind of impact a small church can have. And yet, that church had no "program" for alcoholics.

Similarly, isn't it good for singles to be with couples and families, and not just other singles? Lauren Winner, when she was single some years back, shared a refreshing perspective on her search for a church home:

> When I moved to New York, I visited churches for a year. One of the reasons I settled at the church I joined is that it doesn't have a singles ministry. No one asked me to serve on the worship team of the singles service or teach in the singles Sunday school class; my pastor instead asked me to serve on the education commit-tee. And no one invited me to a singles mixer; instead, I mingle with married friends, engaged friends, wid-owed friends, and other single twentysomethings at the church suppers on Sunday evenings.
>
> I didn't want to be part of a singles ministry because the majority of my needs don't have anything to do with being single. I need prayer. I need to serve others. I need to be held accountable for my sins. And I figure married people need those things, too. I don't want to be segregated with people who, superficially, are just like me.[41]

Tell me: Do you think this lady's walk with God is inhibited because she is in a small church with no ministry focused specifi-cally on singles? Will her friendships be fewer?

Please don't take this too far. I am not saying there shouldn't be ministries that focus on people who are in special-needs situations.

---

[41] Lauren Winner, "Solitary Refinement," *Christianity Today*, June 11, 2001, 30.

I know of many small churches with ministries like these. My hope is that we will see that not being able to provide all kinds of niche ministries is not necessarily a disadvantage—that, in fact, there are advantages to being a small church without specialized ministries.

One large church with many support groups for all kinds of life situations also had a group simply labeled, "Nonspecific Support Group." Small churches have this kind of support group as well. They call it "church."

So, are you ready for that phone call? That call from someone with a special-needs child asking what kind of ministry you have for him or her?

To the church at Galatia, Paul wrote, "There is neither Jew nor Greek, there is neither slave nor free, there is no male and female, for you are all one in Christ Jesus" (Gal. 3:28). These are good words to ponder in what Dean Merrill refers to as our "niche-crazy age."[42] These are good words for the small church to *exploit*!

FOR REFLECTION

1. Share some examples you see in your church of people who are in different life situations ministering to each other.

2. How would you answer the person who inquires about the kinds of ministries your church offers to special-needs children?

---

[42] Dean Merrill, "Not Married-with-Children," *Christianity Today*, July 14, 1997, 34.

CHAPTER NINE

MAXIMIZE THE STRENGTH: MAKE SURE THAT YOU'RE RELATIONAL

Small-church people are probably not overly interested in their pastor's professional skills. They first and foremost want a pastor who is relational. Carl Dudley reinforces this perspective:

> Members of small congregations want the benefit of skilled pastors to serve their churches. But even more important, they want someone whom they feel they can know personally. The most frequent frustration for the laity is the feeling that the pastor, hiding behind that professional polish, is not a real person. They want to know the person; that is their first priority.[43]

Can you see swimming and running in this quote?[44] It is hard to overstate the importance of leaders of small churches having a healthy relational bond with their congregations. Over a span

---

[43] Carl Dudley, *Unique Dynamics of the Small Church* (Bethesda, MD: The Alban Institute, 1977), 71.
[44] See the opening story in Chapter Three.

of many years of observing small churches all across the country, I have found that people in small churches are usually pretty
quick to overlook most shortcomings in their pastors and leaders,
with one prominent exception: they can't get away with not being
relational.

Some Examples

John Smith (not his real name) was a pastor in a small town where
two of his church leaders owned the only two stores in town. The
postmistress was also a member of his church. Pastor Smith was
well educated, his sermons well prepared, and he had a fine family. However, the church asked him to leave. Why? Because he did
not build rapport with the people. He would walk down the town
sidewalk, right past the two stores and post office, and not even
raise his hand in recognition of their presence.[45] Small church
members will forgive their pastor for all kinds of things, but not
for being impersonal.

I heard secondhand that Vance Havner used to tell the story of
embarking upon his first pastorate, a small church, in South Caro-
lina. Several godly pastors had preceded him, but one towered
over the others in the memory of the people; he was the standard
by which all others were measured. Havner was determined to
find the reason. He discovered that his celebrated predecessor was
not a dynamic pulpiteer, somewhat of a bumbling administrator,
and not a commanding leader. One old man in the church cap-
tured this former pastor's appeal in a few words: "He just plain
loved us."

---

[45] This story came from Doran McCarty's book, *Leading the Small Church* (Nashville:
Broadman Press, 1991), 97.

Some time ago, I heard about a research project involving about a dozen pastors.[46] Their preaching ability was judged by several homiletics professors to be roughly equivalent. But when these pastors' congregations were surveyed, the "equal" assessment was turned upside down. The bottom-line conclusion of the project was this: congregations ranked their pastor's preaching according to how well their pastor related to them. Where there were good relationships, they judged their pastor to be a good preacher. Where relationships were lacking, his preaching was judged to be lacking.

A former editor of *Preaching Today* some time ago told me that they would often get submissions from people saying, "Here's a great sermon my pastor preached!" Inevitably, it was an average sermon—very likely preached by a beloved pastor.

Unfortunately, it seems that the "great" pastors in history and up to today have had one thing in common: they are all exceptional preachers. When was the last time a pastor became well known because of his relational skills? What then do we do about the fact that we are so prone to take our cues from the great preachers? What do we do about the fact that most of us pastors are not great preachers? (Pardon me for keeping things real!)

Fortunately, there is encouragement for us from two very important and effective leaders in Bible times. Moses was acutely aware of his weakness: "Oh, my Lord, I am not eloquent. . . . I am slow of speech and of tongue" (Ex. 4:10). People said of the apostle Paul: "his bodily presence is weak, and his speech of no account" (2 Cor. 10:10). And yet, these were two of the most effective leaders in the Bible. Moses and Paul both came to understand "that there was more to carrying out God's purposes, more

---

[46] I heard about this project secondhand, so I cannot verify it. But it certainly rings true.

to being a shepherd of God's people, than the excellent delivery of a message one hour per week."[47]

In no way is this chapter meant to downplay the vital role of the preaching of God's Word. To the contrary, one purpose for this chapter (and Chapter Eleven) is to help increase the impact of preaching for those of us who are not great preachers (I include myself in this group). In the small church where relationships are a high value, the impact of the pastor's preaching depends to a large degree on his commitment to relationships. When pastors establish a strong relational foundation with their congregations, their preaching will be much more well-received and have considerably more impact. This presents a contrast with big churches. In big churches, it is likely that preaching will pave the way for pastoring. In small churches, it is likely that pastoring will pave the way for preaching.

It seems to me that what is true for preaching would also be true for other areas of ministry for small-church pastors and leaders. If a strong relational foundation is established, then small-church people are far more likely to respond to their pastor's vision, counsel, suggestions for change . . . on and on we could go. It is unscripted relational moments that often provide the best opportunities for discipleship and spiritual guidance.

Relationships matter in small churches, especially between leaders and congregations. For how many of us was this an emphasis in our formal pastoral training? David Ray writes:

> The small church frequently expects its minister to be precisely what the seminary often does not train students

---

[47] Brandon O'Brien, *The Strategically Small Church* (Minneapolis: Bethany House Publishers, 2010), 149.

to be, and it does not want what the seminary often does train ministers to be. In a study of rural clergy, one minister wrote: "Ministers succeed or fail . . . not on their ability to preach, nor on their knowledge of history; not on their Biblical understanding, nor any of the scholarly matters, but on the ability to effectively communicate a Christian concern for people."

What they [small-church people] want is not a scholar, therapist, manager, or expert, but a member and a leader of the family. This is not to say small churches do not want or need competent and skilled clergy leadership, but these skills will not be responded to until the door to the church's collective soul is opened with warmth.[48]

The difference here might be swimming and running. A large-church pastor is a dynamic preacher, and this is primarily how he is used of God to mightily impact lives. A small-church pastor might be only an adequate preacher, but he is relational, and it is this combination that is used of God to mightily impact lives. Both accomplish the same purpose, but in different ways.

What If I Am Not Naturally Very Relational?

So you are an introvert, you say? Somewhat curiously, my understanding is that a majority of pastors view themselves as introverts. Or, maybe you are more task-oriented, with a bent toward focusing on sermon preparation, event planning, and vision-casting. Does not having a natural relational bent disqualify you from being a small-church pastor?

---

[48] David Ray, *Small Churches Are the Right Size* (Cleveland: The Pilgrim Press, 1982), 51.

Yours Truly is both an introvert and task-oriented. I am perfectly content with a quiet day in my office. I am not the life of the party. What should the likes of me do?

First, let's not confuse having a natural bent toward solitude and tasks with a dislike for being around people. Though I would almost always pick isolation over crowds, and have even been known to avoid someone in the store when I am shopping, inevitably when I connect with people I enjoy the interaction.

And, let's not confuse loving being around people with loving people. Love is a verb. It's an action. It's a decision. For some of us, it's a decision that requires some intentionality.

What are some possible actions we can take to overcome not being a naturally relational person? Here are some suggestions:

1. ***Pray regularly through your church directory,*** perhaps at a pace whereby you pray for everyone in your congregation at least once a month. Another option is to put names on prayer cards in your car that you revolve through—especially good if you are serving in a remote place where you drive many miles. Intentional praying like this not only brings your church members' needs before God; it also helps bring them to your mind. As you pray, be thinking about what is going on in their lives. This might prompt you to give them a phone call, or send them an email, a text, or a handwritten note. Or, you might decide a personal conversation is warranted, perhaps in the church foyer next Sunday or over a cup of coffee.

2. ***Make a list of people you want to especially be intentional about building relationships with, and how you might do so.*** For me in my rural pastorates, this meant helping ranchers with early morning cattle feeding and

seasonal brandings, hopping on tractors when farmers were out in their fields (there's usually a buddy seat and they are glad for the company!), or riding along with someone to a cattle sale. It might mean making a point of connecting with someone at a ball game (to them it might seem happenstance, but to you it is intentional). It could mean playing a game of Scrabble with an elderly shut-in. Some in your congregation would welcome you bringing coffee or lunch to them at their place of work.

3. *In some contexts, there are relational rhythms that we can tap into.* There may be regular coffee times in the local café—perhaps early morning, mid-morning, or mid-afternoon, all with different groups. There might be a time every morning when folks tend to pick up their mail at the post office. I even know of pastors who often do some of their sermon preparation in local cafés—a ministry of presence, not knowing who might show up and sit with them for a spell. Some have a fairly regular time when they do this, known to folks in the church and community— giving them an opportunity to casually connect with their pastor.

4. *Schedule times on your calendar that you will devote to relationship-building.* For me, having a bent toward being more task-oriented than people-oriented, this scheduling is key. While I may have good intentions when it comes to relationships, a week or two can easily slide by with me doing little in this area unless I schedule it on my calendar. This is a way for a task-oriented person to become more relational. When I was a pastor, I scheduled coffee times on my calendar, scheduled times to visit the

local nursing home, scheduled ball games, etc. And, my wife and I worked out a comfortable hospitality calendar.

Over time, I made a discovery about myself: I enjoy being relational! I would never have learned this had I not been intentional about forging relationships. It was a needed area of growth in my life. And yes, it's still a work in progress.

Soak in this account of a twenty-year ministry anniversary gathering for a small-church pastor, written by Linda, his wife:

> It struck me that no one testified about Jay's incredible delegation skills, his mastery of *Robert's Rules of Order* in committee meetings, his strategic planning, his genius with scheduling. . . . No one said they admire all the reading, studying, and preparing he does. . . . There were stories about the time Jay spent . . . with one of our members. . . . How he accepted, loved, and encouraged a young man after a great failure. . . . They appreciate how he shows up at their kids' sporting events . . .

She then anticipates how her husband will someday be remembered:

> . . . his tombstone . . . will carry some sweet sentimental phrase appropriate for a small-church pastor who sometimes bungles the things that don't matter much, but is an expert in what matters most.[49]

---

[49] Linda Riley, "What Matters in Ministry," *Leadership*, Spring 1995, 103.

Some of you need to read this kind of affirmation, because Jay's name could easily be replaced with yours. Others of us perhaps need some nudging in this area; we need to place a higher value on relationships.

The Bible strongly encourages us to be relational. Being shepherds is our calling (1 Pet. 5:1–4). How can we live this out without being relational? Shepherds don't stand at a distance and tell sheep what to do. Shepherds are not drive-in preachers—shepherds are with their flocks. The sheep know their shepherd, and even know his voice. We simply must make relationships a priority. If we are not growing relationally, we do well to evaluate whether we are growing at all, because being relational is part and parcel of how God created each of us.

To paraphrase 1 Corinthians 13: If I do all the other things of ministry but have not relationships, I will just be a noisy gong to those in my congregation and community.

FOR REFLECTION

1. Are you an extrovert or an introvert?

2. Would your spouse and/or people in your congregation say that you are an extrovert or an introvert?

3. Are you tilted more toward being a people person or a task person? What might you do to bring these two more into balance?

4. How will you someday be remembered by your congregation?

CHAPTER TEN

MAXIMIZE THE STRENGTH: DESIGN WORSHIP SERVICES TO REFLECT THE RELATIONAL BENT OF YOUR CONGREGATION

Perhaps small churches feel most inferior to large when comparing worship services. Want better music? Go to a large church. Want better sound and lighting? Want things to run more smoothly? Want better preaching? Go to a large church.

We're back to swimming vs. running. If small churches look to big churches to determine the standard for a "good" worship service, they will inevitably fall short. Might there be a way for small churches to have worship services that are just as glorifying to God, and just as edifying, meaningful, and impactful to those in attendance?

I'd like to suggest that a good way for this to happen is by designing the worship services to reflect the relational strength of the congregation. Let me offer words that describe worship services designed with this relational bent in mind: personal, spontaneous, participative, folksy, informal, intergenerational.

The risk of trying to fulfill descriptive words like these is taking them too far—to the point where worship services might also be described by words such as chaotic and unplanned. Most small-church attenders want enough planning to keep their services from matching these descriptions, but they also want the kind of informal and unstructured folksiness one would expect when a family gets together.

Wisdom follows the ancient advice "Know thyself," and then tailors the church's worship services accordingly. In this chapter and the next, I'd like to offer some suggestions. Of course, you will need to put these through your own ecclesiastical and cultural grids. Some will likely not be appropriate for your context.

Welcome, Greeting, and Announcements Time

This time in the worship service is a wonderful opportunity to plug into relationships. As you do so, think about how you can add a personal touch:

> "It's Bob and Lucy's fiftieth wedding anniversary. Lucy, you are a saint for sticking with Bob all these years!"

> "We're excited to let you know that the Smiths welcomed little Joella last Friday. Here's a picture. Isn't she a keeper?"

> "Congratulations to the high school volleyball team for making it to State. Didn't Lindsey do a great job out there on the court?"

> "What a wonderful community festival we had this week. I saw many of you helping out in lots of different ways. How great it was to see our church in action in the community!"

> "Today is Jeremy's graduation. Many of us remember Jeremy crawling under our pews and now he's going

to be walking across the stage. Jeremy, you have turned into a fine young man!"

"Our Vacation Bible School starts this evening. I have been so impressed as different ones have been in the church this week setting up for this. I could tell they were having lots of fun, and that they are looking forward to welcoming a pack of kids here tonight. Thank you all for creating such a wonderful atmosphere for our children!"

For many small churches, an informal greet-your-neighbor time is a highlight in the service. I've been in churches where five minutes or more was given to this. For small-church people, this is more than a perfunctory greeting time; it is a time to catch up on what's happening in each other's lives. It's also a time for the congregation to care for one another. So much can happen in just a few moments of conversation. A pastor friend of mine calls this "the ministry of walking around."

This part of the service should not be rushed. As it unfolds, I highly doubt that folks like Bob and Lucy, Jeremy and his parents, and the girls on the volleyball team will be sitting there thinking, "I wish I was in a large church." These kinds of personal touches are not likely to happen in large churches.

Sharing and Praying Time

How often do you hear people prayed for by name in a large church?

In my visits to hundreds of small churches across the country, I have observed some really meaningful sharing and praying times. This part of the service is an opportunity for the family to share news with each other, express gratitude, share concerns, celebrate joys, etc. This is prime time to "encourage the fainthearted, help the weak . . . rejoice always, pray without ceasing, give thanks" (1 Thess. 5:14–18).

Years ago, my family was on the receiving end of this kind of personal touch. Our daughter Charissa had broken her arm at school on a Friday afternoon. If you're going to break an arm, I suggest not doing it on a Friday afternoon! The emergency room put Charissa's arm in a temporary cast and scheduled surgery for Monday. My wife and I groaned about having to wait a couple of days for the healing to begin. Unknown to us, another kind of healing was in the works. On Sunday morning, our pastor invited all the children to come up front and sit on the steps. He asked Charissa to sit beside him. Then he said, "We want to pray for Charissa, because she is having surgery tomorrow." Maybe it wouldn't be such a bad idea after all to plan a broken arm for a Friday afternoon! My wife and I were grateful that we were in a small church that offered a personal touch.

The sharing and praying time in the small church's worship service can be amazing. Or not. I've been in situations where Gladys raises her hand and everyone rolls their eyes because she never lets a week go by without sharing, and usually she goes on and on. Or, situations that become an "organ recital"—when almost exclusively, people's ailments are rehearsed for everyone to hear. Or, situations where information is provided about someone who is so distant that it's hard to connect with the concern— e.g., "My neighbor's got a cousin who lives in California who was in a terrible accident."

Very likely, some training for this special time of the service would be helpful—perhaps not formal training as much as gentle reminders from time to time as you begin this part of the worship service. Reminders to stick with prayer requests that are not too far removed from the church family. Reminders that encourage brevity. Reminders that help our people differentiate between prayer requests and gossip. And, reminders that help our congregation understand that this isn't just a prayer time for physical needs. Much of this informal training can happen simply by the pastor and other leaders setting an example in their praying. Pray for such things as unity, for the youth to have a good testimony at school, for people to come to Christ, for strong marriages, for God to help us be edifying in our conversations, etc. A good option from time to time is praying prayers of the Bible—personalizing them for your congregation.

Worship Music

We do well to ask: What makes worship worshipful? Hopefully a key element of our answer is: when it is focused on God. With this in mind, it could be easier to attain authentic worship in a small church than in a big church.

Some time ago, I had a conversation with a woman who grew up in a large church. She had married a farmer and was now a member of a small church. She had just returned from her first visit back home since her marriage. While there, she had attended her former church. Reflecting, she said to me: "It seemed like such a production. I never noticed this when I was living there. As I sat in the service, I wondered to myself, *Do people need all this glitz to worship? My country church is so humble. They don't attend for a show.*"

While I am certain there are many who attend large churches who enter into authentic worship each Sunday—and equally certain there are many in small churches who do not practice authentic worship—it seems to me that the temptation is greater in large churches to focus much of worship on the attenders rather than on God. Large churches tend to place a higher priority on such things as talent, excellence, choosing songs and music styles that appeal to the members, and having top-notch accoutrements (lighting, sound equipment, projectors, musical instruments, etc.). How can small churches possibly measure up to these standards? But, this doesn't mean their worship in any way need be inferior. We do well to remind ourselves that worship at its best acknowledges God's worth "in spirit" (John 4:24)—material things are of secondary importance.

Years ago, Soren Kierkegaard, Danish philosopher and theologian, offered a perspective on worship that is refreshing and liberating for small-church attenders. He compared worship to drama, pointing out that with drama we have actors. Drawing a parallel to worship, he said that the actors rightfully should be the congregation. With drama, there are prompters. With worship, he said the prompters should be the worship leaders up front. With drama, there is an audience. With worship, the audience should be God (see 1 Chron. 16:29; Ps. 29:2).

Think of the implications of this analogy. The focal point in worship should not be the prompters—i.e., the leaders up front. In fact, if they are doing their job well, they will barely be noticed. The audience—God—is focused on the actors, and in worship the actors are the congregation. How often do we get this mixed up? We think worship is something that happens up front, which the rest of the congregation sits back and enjoys. In reality, the best worship happens when the congregation is fully engaged. This plays right into the strengths of the small church that gathers as a family and values every member's participation.

Making It Practical

From this, there are a treasure-trove of applications and encouragements for small-church attenders. Let me highlight a few:

Perhaps excellence should yield to participation. God is far more exalted when the entire congregation is engaged in worship than when members are largely spectators of worship. In no way am I saying that we shouldn't give God our best worship, but for some of us, our best is a "joyful noise."

It could be that we need to redefine excellence. Shawn McMullen helps us with this:

> I didn't coin the phrase, but in the church I serve we often operate according to the "good enough" principle. It's natural to assume that the talent pool is smaller in smaller churches. As a result, members of smaller churches with average (or even below average) talent often have opportunities to participate in public worship and ministry in ways that would be denied them in larger churches. This doesn't mean we shouldn't strive for excellence in all we do, but it does mean that in the smaller church, a genuine heart and a willingness to serve are often valued above skill level and professional presentation. In addition, folks in smaller churches are notorious for their tolerance. Those who lead and serve even with modest abilities in the smaller church can expect to be loved, accepted, and encouraged.[50]

This isn't an excuse for lack of preparation or laziness. It's tough for a congregation to worship when they are squirming because their "prompters" (a.k.a. worship leaders) are ill-prepared. But, we

---

[50] Shawn McMullen, *The Power of the Smaller Church* (Cincinnati: Standard Publishing, 2007), 20–21.

need to be wary of mercilessly pushing for excellence because of our misguided need to impress people.

The best worship leader may not be the person with the most musical talent. The best worship leader is the one who has a knack for drawing worship out of the congregation.

Small-church pastor Bill Giovannetti learned this lesson the hard way. He wrote about choosing a music leader based upon what he felt was a need to improve the quality of music. Soon he noted that the congregation had moved from being worshippers to observers. He discerned that at the root of the problem was the fact that he had chosen a musician rather than a worship leader. It takes a leader to inspire a congregation to enter wholeheartedly into worship.[51]

A good worship leader in a small church will tap into its relational strength. He will see himself as the leader of a family that has gathered for worship. Understanding this, he will keep things informal and folksy, and maintain a good balance between preparation and spontaneity.

Years ago, my large-church background prompted me to push for excellence during our church's annual Christmas celebrations. My motivation, in part, was to impress outsiders who might be visiting. After a couple of years of this, a discerning member of my congregation suggested that maybe we should rearrange the seating in our sanctuary around the keyboard and make it a family time of singing Christmas carols together. What a joyful and beautiful evening it turned out to be!

"Paint with the colors God gives you," and make it the mantra of your music selection. Often in large churches, the mantra

---

[51] Bill Giovannetti, "Great Worship with Modest Means," *Leadership*, Spring 1994, 52–57.

for music selection is a particular music style. They may offer a service with a contemporary music style, a more traditional music style, or a style that reflects a certain genre (e.g., southern gospel, classical, soul). Contrast this to the approach Lee Eclov came to for his church:

> I was thinking one day of a painter.... "Wait," I said, "I need more colors than that.".... Then God, our art instructor, says, "I've given you all you need to portray Christ through your church. Just paint with the colors I gave you."
>
> Instead of trying to be contemporary, blended, or traditional in worship, we try to be *us*.... Many churches choose their worship style and music in order to appeal to the kinds of people they want to draw. Many use only their best musicians. I get that. But we have decided not to do it that way. We decided that, whenever we can, we will use the people God gives us, as many of them as possible, regardless of whether they play a bass or a bassoon.[52]

With maximum participation being our goal, music selection should be narrowed to songs that are more playable and singable. This can vary, depending upon where you are located and who is in your congregation. Some songs are difficult for musicians to play, which in turn makes it difficult for singers to sing. Some songs have melodies that are difficult for average singers to sing. Some congregations sing certain genres of music better than others. Certainly familiar songs are sung the best, though it is important to introduce new songs from time to time.

[52] Lee Eclov, *Pastoral Graces: Reflections on the Care of Souls* (Chicago: Moody Publishers, 2012), 92–93.

"The colors God gives you" includes people of varying ages. It means being intentional about making worship an intergenerational experience. We should use people of all ages on the platform[53]—as instrumentalists and as vocal leaders. We should select worship songs that span the ages of those in our congregation. I've been in small churches that weave children's songs into the music selections, along with old hymns and contemporary songs.

In my library is a book titled *Worship Is a Verb*.[54] This summarizes the important principle that the best worship happens when we are participants, not spectators. The apostle Paul talks about "each one" participating in the worship services (1 Cor. 14:26).

Years ago, Fred Smith, the son of a small-church pastor, decided he wanted to write an article on the advantages of small churches. For preparation, he attended a number of small-church worship services. Afterward he observed, "I was impressed that the service wasn't held for the membership but by them."[55]

The actors: the congregation. The prompters: the worship leaders. The audience: God. Small churches are ideal for living this out!

Special Happenings

It is always good to be thinking how we can provide a personal touch to all aspects of the worship services. This includes special occasions.

If appropriate in your context, perhaps a dad can baptize his child. Or, maybe the one who led the person to Christ can do the

---

[53] I use the word "platform" deliberately. With the congregation being the "actors" in worship, the "stage" is where they are sitting. This careful choice of words can be one reminder, of many, of the small church's philosophy of worship.

[54] Robert E. Webber, *Worship Is a Verb* (Waco, TX: Word Books, 1985).

[55] Fred Smith, "The Unique Role of the Small Church," *Leadership*, Fall 1991, 86.

baptizing. I find it interesting that in most traditions we apply the Great Commission to everyone except the baptizing part, which we reserve for clergy only.

Regardless of who does the baptizing, this is a wonderful opportunity to make the occasion highly personal. Those being baptized might share their conversion story, or a few words of testimony about what their new life in Christ means to them. The one doing the baptizing or perhaps someone else in the congregation might also say some well-chosen words about the one being baptized—perhaps how their faith is encouraging those who are watching, or how already their life is touching others. Perhaps a special friend or family member can pray for the one being baptized.

One pastor tells of how baptisms happen in his small church. He invites "everyone who wants to see what's going on" to come closer. What follows is quite a picture: children, a mother holding a baby, friends, aunts and uncles, cousins, and grandparents all gather around. The pastor asks if the children know what is going on. Several of them aren't sure. Then, one of the older girls chimes in: "We're going to baptize Joe!" (Notice the theology: "We're," not "You're.") The whole congregation laughs together. They are obviously enjoying the occasion.

"That's right," the pastor says. "And, what will we baptize Joe with?" The children look at each other, wondering if this is a trick question. Finally, someone says, "Water!" Everyone laughs again. "And, do you think there's anything special about this water?" he asks. There is a long silence. Obviously, the children are thinking, as are the adults. Finally, one young boy says, "Looks like regular water to me." The other children and adults wait to see if the boy will be corrected by the pastor.

"That's right, Seth," says the pastor. "It's not magic water; it's just regular water that came out of the faucet. Go ahead and touch it if you'd like." Several of them dip their fingers in the water. "Ooh, it's cold!" one girl exclaims. "It's wet!" says a little boy. "Of course it's wet—it's water!" says another boy. There's more laughter.

Everyone is enjoying watching the children discover what baptism is all about. "We don't have special water for baptisms," continues the pastor, "because it's not needed." He goes on to explain. Then, he baptizes. And with each baptism, the people clap. A baptism, like a barn raising, provides another shared experience for the community of believers, both adults and children.[56]

Child dedications, graduations, weddings, and funerals are other wonderful opportunities to be highly personal. Perhaps along with the pastor, fellow church members can be invited to share memories, or words of blessing, affirmation, and support.

Hopefully you are envisioning the small church's relational strength being on display whenever the church gathers together. Might this relational bent also be on display when preaching? Keep reading.

FOR REFLECTION

1. What would you say should not be changed about your church's worship services?

2. Did this chapter prompt you to think of some improvements that might be made to your church's worship services? If so, what are they?

3. How does your church "paint with the colors God has given you"? Think beyond the worship services to other ministries of your church.

---

[56] This story was adapted from Steve Burt, *Activating Leadership in the Small Church* (Valley Forge, PA: Judson Press, 1988), 17–19.

CHAPTER ELEVEN

MAXIMIZE THE STRENGTH: TAP INTO YOUR CONGREGATION'S RELATIONAL BENT WITH YOUR PREACHING

Perhaps questions have come to mind as you've thought about preaching in your small church, like:

- Might there be some things that could be done with the layout of the sanctuary that enhance preaching?
- Might there be some ways to tailor my sermon content so that it better fits our small-church context?
- Might there be some distinct characteristics of my sermon delivery style?
- What if I don't have the preaching ability of large-church pastors? Does this mean my preaching will not have as much impact?

Context consciously and subconsciously impacts preaching, doesn't it? If you are Christ walking through the countryside, stopping and preaching wherever you have opportunity, wherever people gather—sometimes small numbers sometimes large, often outdoors—would your preaching be different than inside a building? If you are in a massive cathedral-like building, might you preach differently than if you are in a small-church, multipurpose gathering room? If you are preaching in a marketplace like Paul in Acts 17, would your preaching be different? If your listeners are highly educated, might this impact your preaching?

Let me share what I like to call "The Five I's of Small-Church Preaching."

Individualize

Your preaching is delivered to people within a specific zip code. This means your sermons should be tailored for this particular context, especially the illustrations and applications. Don't talk about Uber if people in your area don't know what it is or if it's not available. Rather, use examples that are peculiar to your context. When preaching on Jonah, ask: What is Nineveh to us here? When talking about the kindness Boaz shows to Ruth, ask: Who are the outsiders here? When preaching on James's verses about planning for tomorrow, ask: What does this mean for the agricultural workers in our congregation?

If you craft your sermon well, you probably won't be able to preach it anywhere else. It should be individualized for your context. To do this, you must know your context well. Contextualization is another reason why it is so important that we preachers develop relationships with our people. It is impossible for us to tailor sermons if we don't know our people—know how they think and know about their experiences of life.

Intimate

In a small church, sermons are not addressed to a crowd but to people with names that are known to the preacher. These are people who also know each other well. This intimacy helps us individualize our sermons, as stated above—a wonderful strength of small-church preaching. But some cautions are in order.

If you're not careful, the intimacy of a small church can become a weakness. Because you know your people well, it is easy for you to see them in the sermon text that you are preparing for Sunday—easy to think, *I've been wanting an opportunity to talk to Joe about this very thing, and here it is in the text. This must be God's way of saying the time is now!*

A rule of thumb: the smaller the congregation, the greater the risk that its members will think their pastor is preaching at them, resulting in a much greater chance for them to take offense to his preaching. Familiarity can be particularly difficult to navigate when texts address specific situations that certain individuals in your church are going through, such as drunkenness or divorce. If so, you do well to choose your words carefully. It does help if you are committed to expository preaching through books of the Bible.[57] Then your congregation knows that you aren't targeting anyone in particular with a text.

It is also helpful to use the word "we" as much as possible in sermons—not "when *you* face temptation" but "when *we* face temptation." This should probably be done even when it's not

---

[57] Tim Keller, in *Preaching: Communicating Faith in an Age of Skepticism* (New York: Penguin, 2015), defines expository preaching this way: "Expository preaching grounds the message in the text so that all the sermon's points are the points in the text, and it majors in the text's major ideas" (32).

something you personally struggle with. Nehemiah was a great example. He confessed the sins of his fellow Jews, using the word "we" even though he was not even alive when they had committed those sins (Neh. 1:6–7).[58] It might also help to say something like, "While we know some who are struggling with this very thing, we also know that it could happen to any of us."

It is good to be careful about making even veiled references to people in your church and community. People will have an uncanny way of figuring out who you are talking about. Be careful about saying something like, "The other day I stopped to help someone who had pulled off the road with car trouble. While waiting for the tow truck, this person shared about how so many things in her life have been going wrong of late." If we live in a small community, chances are good that several listening saw this happen and will know who we are referring to. Worse, they probably won't be shy to share that person's name with others.

A preacher might say, "I was talking to someone this past week who is having struggles in his marriage." People will think, *I saw Tom's car in the church parking lot last Thursday. I bet it was him.* Or we might say, "I was talking to someone who is struggling with anger issues." People will think, *I bet that's Angie. She is constantly venting.*

You do not want to make people feel like their pastor is constantly watching and judging their every move. You don't want people to worry that the happenings in their lives, especially their struggles, will end up as sermon illustrations. For sure, you should never use anyone as a negative example. The one exception to this might be the preacher—there might be a lot that others can learn from our mistakes! If you have a positive story to tell

---

[58] Jeremiah did the same in his intercessory prayer in Jeremiah 14:7–9, as did Daniel in Daniel 9:3–19. The psalmist repeatedly used "we" as well in Psalm 106.

about someone in your church or community, it would probably be good to ask their permission, because some people do not want to be talked about in public.

What I've just said about people in general is doubly important for the pastor's family. You do not want your wife and children to be nervous about coming to church every Sunday, wondering if they are going to be used as a sermon illustration. Fun, harmless stories about your family might be fine. For example, you might have a cute story to tell about your one-year-old learning how to walk. There may be rare occasions when it is appropriate to get permission from one of your family members to tell a story that involves them. But "rare" is the operative word.

Some time ago, I was visiting with the new widow of a highly respected small-town pastor. Reflecting on her husband's ministry, she said to me, "He never preached at anyone."

Intergenerational

In a small church, it's likely that you're preaching to a wide span of ages, perhaps from cradle to almost grave. Yours is not a niche congregation—not a particular generation. This needs to be kept in mind as you prepare sermons. It is good to be intentional about preaching to everyone. In particular, it is good to shy away from the temptation to preach primarily to people like yourself, people in a similar life stage as yours.

As you prepare sermons, you do well to pretend that there are all kinds of people sitting across your desk asking, "What are you going to say to me?" A child is asking this question. A young, single adult. Married couples with children. Empty nesters. Seniors, including widows and widowers.

With certain subjects and texts, it is good to be especially careful about word choice, particularly as it relates to children. It is good to be careful how you talk about Mary, mother of Christ, being a virgin; or of getting too graphic when talking about animal sacrifices in the Old Testament.

When your preaching is upstaged by a crying baby or a wandering toddler, see this as an important moment. Avoid showing or expressing annoyance. Instead, see this as an opportunity to say a word about how wonderful it is to have young children in the congregation, and to have families together in the worship service.

Informal

Most small-church people view the Sunday morning service as a family gathering. This means that formal, stiff, polished preaching will seem like a foreigner in the room. Listeners will appreciate a more folksy, down-home style of delivery. They probably appreciate a delivery that is more conversational than "preachy." Why is it that we preachers are so inclined to talk differently when we stand behind a pulpit or lectern?

It is good to avoid stuffy, academic sermons—no matter how much good information you gleaned from your studying. Your people probably don't care about these nuggets as much as you do. Sometimes, how academic information is presented can make all the difference in the world. For example, when talking about the lack of an article in the Greek in John 1:1, it could be incorporated into a story of how this came up in conversation with a person who is a Jehovah's Witness or Mormon.

It is good to think about how the atmosphere of your preaching can reinforce this informal strength. Does the room scream stiffness or warmth? Do you stand on a significantly raised platform? Is there a barrier between you and the congregation (like a waist-high wall across the front of the platform)? Is there considerable distance between you and where the congregation is sitting? Do you stand behind a large, imposing pulpit? I'm not suggesting that you immediately change some of these things, because that could get you into trouble. But perhaps there are some gradual tweaks that you can make to the physical layout of your sanctuary, or wherever your preaching takes place, that will enhance this small-church strength of informality.

Involved

There's a rule of thumb: the smaller the place, the higher the level of involvement. If it's a small school, there's a higher percentage of involvement of students in the school's sports, clubs, and music programs. Similarly, small churches have a much higher percentage of involvement than their large-church counterparts.

How might this be reflected in your preaching, particularly your sermon delivery? One way is to involve your congregation in the sermon. This may not be for everyone or every situation, but it is something I encourage you to consider.

Those of us with homiletics training were probably taught a one-way preaching delivery method—a method that, if we think about it, might be more fitting for a large-church context. I want to encourage you to think about adjusting your preaching style in accordance with the size of your congregation.

Much of Jesus's preaching was delivered to small numbers of people. His preaching style in these kinds of situations is instructive. Often people would gather around Him as He spoke. Often, He did not limit Himself to one-way communication. Often His teaching and preaching were highly interactive. A message on faith in Matthew 18 began with a question from the audience, followed by Christ setting a child on His lap and then preaching a sermon. His teaching on divorce in Matthew 19 was in response to questions from the crowd. Christ told stories. He shared object lessons. He knelt and wrote in the sand while people gathered around. He asked questions. He answered questions.

In the small church that I pastored years ago in Nebraska, I often asked questions during the sermon, or allowed time for the congregation to ask me questions or make comments. At times, I asked someone in the congregation (usually ahead of time) to share for just a couple of minutes about an experience I knew they had gone through that mirrored the teaching of the text. For example, a wife shared about how God worked through her husband's cancer. Sometimes, if someone in our congregation had some expertise on a topic or situation addressed in our text, I'd call and ask them questions that helped me better understand the text. For instance, the Bible is full of agricultural imagery and my church was loaded with ranchers and farmers. They loved the opportunity to be my teacher! Often, as I was sharing my newly discovered information in my sermon, I'd be sure to name the person who enlightened me.

After a message on marriage, I opened the floor up for discussion. What followed was something better than I could ever have scripted. A middle-aged, divorced man spoke up: "If I had known twenty years ago some of the things that were shared in the message this morning, my first marriage wouldn't have failed. I hope the teenagers here were listening, and that you young couples will heed the principles in the text so that your marriages won't end like mine did." A hush fell over the congregation. There was not a dry eye in the room. My preaching wasn't nearly as impactful as this man's comments!

Another time, assurance of salvation was the topic of my message. Afterward, as I gave time for our congregation to respond, a lady who had for years struggled with assurance said, "This issue is really important. I know I didn't start growing as a Christian until I settled it. I kept looking back on my salvation instead of forward to my need for growth." That week, I received a note from another lady in our congregation, thanking me for the message which she said had been a significant help to her. I suspect that the greatest help came from the sharing of one of her friends.

Before we leave this topic of small-church preaching, I want to pass along a piece of advice that was given to me years ago that has proven time and again to be especially helpful: do the bulk of your sermon preparation well ahead of time, perhaps six weeks or so. This advice is particularly helpful for solo pastors, because you never know what might suddenly and unexpectedly require your time. And, because you are so relationally connected to people in your church and community, these unplanned interruptions and distractions (also known as opportunities for ministry!) can be much more time-consuming.

When I was a solo pastor, I was a member of the volunteer emergency squad. An ambulance run, almost always with only seconds' notice, would often take four hours or more out of my day. A sudden crisis might come up, all of a sudden you end up with two funerals in the same week, or you get sick during the week. When situations like these happen, working ahead means no worries about Sunday's sermon!

This simple piece of advice regarding sermon preparation has proven to be one of my greatest stress-relievers in ministry. If an unexpected situation came up, I didn't have to worry about finding time to get my sermon done before Sunday. And, if the crisis spilled over into several days and I didn't have any time for sermon preparation that week, I was still five weeks ahead in my sermon preparation. When situations like these happened, I was much more relaxed and able to minister with less of an anxious presence, because I wasn't worried about an unfinished sermon that needed my attention.

How, you ask, did I get six weeks ahead with sermon preparation? It took a couple of years. Every time I had a Sunday off from preaching, I went ahead and prepared a sermon anyway.

There are other benefits to preparing sermons ahead of time. One is that it gives time for your sermons to percolate. Inevitably, thoughts and ideas will come to mind that improve the content of your preaching. Another is that should an issue suddenly come up in your community that also comes up in your sermon text, then your people will know (assuming they know you do sermon preparation ahead of time) that you didn't deliberately craft a sermon that addresses the current issue. Another benefit to preparing sermons in advance is that it gives those who are in charge of the music some time to select songs that have tie-ins to the text.

Some of us small-church pastors may not have the preaching talent of the giants. But could it be that if we adjust our approach, our preaching might have just as much impact?

FOR REFLECTION

1. Which of the five "I's" of small-church preaching comes naturally for you? Which is a struggle?

2. What in this chapter would you say is not for you and/or your church?

3. A repeat question from Chapter Three for you to ponder again as you near the end of this book: If you never find yourself ministering in a medium- or large-sized church, how would you feel about yourself as a pastor/leader and as a person?

A FAITHFUL SMALL-CHURCH PASTOR

The fact that you have read this far tells me that you care deeply about small-church ministry and want to do it well. Do you know that you have a kindred spirit in the New Testament? My hope is to leave you inspired by his example of faithfulness.

In Chapter Two, I introduced you to the small church at Colossae, located in a small town that was declining in population. The apostle Paul, in his letter to this congregation, begins by heaping words of praise on them. He calls them "faithful." He tells them he is "thankful" for them. He commends them for their "faith" and "love." He takes time to craft words about the preeminence of Christ that some say are the most eloquent of all the words in all of his letters. This eloquence reminds me of a small-church pastor who once told me that he works as hard at preparing sermons for a handful as he does for a hundred.

This small church is not viewed by Paul as second-rate. There's no hint of him saying, "If you could just be like the big church in Jerusalem (or today, Chicago). . .". He has enormous praise for this church. He sees many good qualities there. They may not have a forty-acre campus, a multimillion-dollar budget, or multiple services attended by thousands. Their pastor may not have ten thousand followers on Twitter. But these kinds of things don't seem to matter to Paul.

Paul saves his highest praise for the lead elder or pastor of the Colossian church. By the way, do you know his name? I'm guessing you don't—just like the names of most of us who work in small-church ministry are not known beyond the city limit sign or county line. Just like the ones Donald McCullough describes in an unattributed quote that I have hanging on my office wall:

> We would do well to remember that the church, for the most part, is nourished by unknown pastors who stay at it, day by day, in ordinary congregations of sinners who, by grace and prodding, are being slowly cajoled into sainthood.

Epaphras was living out this quote in Colossae. He was the one who nurtured the wonderful qualities which Paul highlights in the opening words of his letter. Paul calls Epaphras "beloved." He has affection for him. He calls him a "fellow servant." There's no hint of condescension, no viewing Epaphras as a lesser guy because he is in a small place. Paul views Epaphras as an equal in the ministry—a fellow servant.

Years ago, when I was a young pastor in Corn, Oklahoma (population less than five hundred), Warren Wiersbe spoke at our church. He was the author of nearly two hundred books, including commentaries on every book of the Bible, and an internationally known preacher. Soon, I received a letter from him (this was before email) . . . then another. We corresponded for more than thirty years, until God promoted him to heaven. After several years, he added this PS to his letter: "The next time you write, please make

'Dear Dr. and Mrs. Wiersbe' into 'Dear Warren and Betty.' It takes a lot less energy." What was Warren doing? Treating me like a fellow servant, an equal—though his ministry was exponentially bigger. He was treating me with the same respect that he had for people in much larger places.

Paul has some more words of praise for Epaphras: "He is a faithful minister of Christ on your behalf" (Col. 1:7). Can you imagine any better words an unknown elder or pastor might read from an internationally known Christian? Can a small-church pastor be considered just as faithful in Christ's service as a person in a bigger place? Are the words, "Well done, good and faithful servant" proportionate to size or place?

There are hints in Colossians as to why Paul considered Epaphras to be a faithful man—at least five in this short letter.

A Faithful Discipler

First, Colossians 1:6–7 tells us that this small group of believers had "learned" from Epaphras. The word here is derived from the word "disciple." Disciplers pour their lives into people; they invest in people—in a steady, systematic, and disciplined way (the words "discipline" and "disciple" come from the same root). Discipleship isn't usually very glamorous. The believers in Colossae were growing because week-in and week-out Epaphras was a faithful discipler. It's one of the reasons Paul calls Epaphras "faithful."

Interestingly, the Navigators, one of the most well-known discipleship ministries of our day, named perhaps their best-known discipleship program the "2:7 Program." Do you know where 2:7 is found? It's striking that one of the most respected discipleship ministries of our day has tipped their hat to the ministry of a first-century small church located in a small town!

Here are some questions for you to ponder: Could it be that a church smaller in size has an advantage when it comes to discipling? Can a pastor effectively disciple someone if he doesn't know their name? If he doesn't spend any personal time with them? If he doesn't rub shoulders with them during the week? How different is it in a context of social intimacy, where the discipler's life can be an example to others, where you are doing life together, iron sharpening iron?

I know that many of you reading this are pouring your lives into others, some of you for many years. Maybe you don't always think of this as a discipling ministry, but it is. If I am describing you, I want to thank you for being faithful like Epaphras!

A Faithful Servant

Colossians 1:7 reveals a second evidence of Epaphras' faithfulness: it says he was a "servant" (Paul repeats this in 4:12). I don't have to tell you that folks in small churches have ample opportunities to exhibit this quality! A lot of what you do is barely noticed— things like cleaning, sweeping and shoveling walkways, picking up litter, mowing, typing church bulletins, setting up rooms for special events . . . on and on it goes. Your servant spirit often extends beyond the church building, to doing all kinds of things for folks in the church and community, like taking people to the doctor, preparing meals for those who've just gotten home from the hospital, helping a single mom with repairs around the house . . . the examples are endless. It is doing these kinds of things in obscurity, where no one is watching and where perhaps few express appreciation, without calling attention to yourself, and without complaining, that gives evidence that you are a servant. Being a servant is another characteristic of a faithful person in the eyes of God. If this describes you, I want to thank you for being faithful like Epaphras!

A Faithful Prayer Warrior

Colossians 4:12 says Epaphras was "always struggling on your behalf in his prayers." The word here means *agonizing*. It is the same word used for our Lord's praying in the garden of Gethsemane (Luke 22:44). Paul says Epaphras prayed this way "always"—often agonizing in prayer for his little group of believers and for his community. If I'm describing you, I want to thank you for being a faithful prayer warrior like Epaphras!

A Faithful Worker

Colossians 4:13 says Epaphras "has worked hard for you"—i.e., for this small group of believers. When you work hard in your obscure place where no one is watching, and perhaps few are aware of the many hours you are putting into ministry, God sees you as being faithful. I know that many of you pour yourselves into the work. "All in" is another way to say it. God bless you for your faithfulness!

Faithful to Sound Doctrine

When folks in the Colossian church had some significant doctrinal questions, Epaphras took it seriously. Reading through Colossians, you can see that this church was not clear on their understanding of Christology. Epaphras was so committed to sound doctrine that apparently, he traveled all the way to Rome to get counsel from Paul.[59] This is a distance of more than a thousand miles, some of it by sea—quite a feat for that day! Epaphras so loved his people,

---

[59] While we are not absolutely certain of all that took place, this seems to be a pretty accurate scenario. Colossians 1:7 indicates Epaphras had a face-to-face conversation with Paul. In 4:12, Paul says that Epaphras, who apparently was with him, "greets you." In Philemon 23, he says that Epaphras was with him in prison. (Philemon was a prominent resident of Colossae.)

and so wanted to protect them from doctrinal error that would hinder their spiritual development and ultimately destroy the church, that he went to great lengths to keep this from happening. This stirred up enormous respect in Paul for Epaphras, leading him to conclude that Epaphras was a faithful church leader. He would say the same for you in your meticulous striving to be true to God's Word.

Obviously, Epaphras was not a crop-duster preacher. He wasn't the kind of pastor who swoops in on Sunday, drops his load, and then flies away. He had boots on the ground, doing life with his congregation, a shepherd who day-in and day-out was with his sheep. This is what a faithful elder/pastor looks like!

The small church can be a wonderful place to grow in Christ. It can be a wonderful place to be used of God. It can be a wonderful place with many strengths to *exploit*. It can be a wonderful place to leverage its relational strength into other strengths. It can be a wonderful place in which to be found faithful! God bless you, faithful small-church leader!